The Sunday Book

THE
SUNDAY BOOK

Michael Trussler

Palimpsest Press
1171 Eastlawn Ave.
Windsor, Ontario, N8S 3J1
www.palimpsestpress.ca

Printed and bound in Canada
Cover design and book typography by Ellie Hastings
Edited by Jim Johnstone
Copyedited by Theo Hummer

Palimpsest Press would like to thank the Canada Council for the Arts
and the Ontario Arts Council for their support of our publishing program. We also acknowledge the assistance of the Government of Ontario
through the Ontario Book Publishing Tax Credit.

LIBRARY AND ARCHIVES CANADA CATALOGUING IN PUBLICATION

TITLE: The Sunday book / Michael Trussler.
NAMES: Trussler, Michael, 1960- author.
DESCRIPTION: Essays.
IDENTIFIERS: Canadiana (print) 20220143323
            Canadiana (ebook) 2022014334X

ISBN 9781990293153 (SOFTCOVER)
ISBN 9781990293160 (EPUB)
ISBN 9781990293177 (PDF)

CLASSIFICATION: LCC PS8639.R89 S96 2022 | DDC C814/.6—DC23

To Philip and my family.

TABLE OF CONTENTS

Wherever I step I am stepping into a place that was just finished at the moment I arrived.
—Fanny Howe, *The Winter Sun: Notes on a Vocation*

BODHISATTVA ON A BICYCLE

Appearing from nowhere, the world sometimes holds up various mirrors. It takes luck to glimpse them, and then to see what's gathered inside. There are so many species of time, each in need of protection. The baroque thuds on the raw.

*

Cryptic, sometimes gnomic, language is one such mirror. Another is anxiety. Because mine keeps worsening, a counselor advised me to take a meditation class with a teacher he knew. She's Buddhist, someone with a smoothly worn presence, and our group, mostly women, met twice weekly. Each of us was there for therapeutic reasons, though it quickly became clear that some were suffering more acutely than others, their pain having to do with severe illness, serial miscarriages, and death. Each class we would practice meditating together for a half hour: sometimes it was like entering a room adjacent to ourselves, the reverberations from a small brass gong the door that opened to let us inside and then the same sound the door closing behind us. Almost always, it was impossibly difficult. To concentrate on even three consecutive breaths was as challenging as it is for a child to keep balanced on a bike for the first time. Each class, we were reminded that the ego is transitory. For this therapy to succeed, it seemed necessary to allow for the Buddhist rejection of a continuous, stable self. This position is reasonable, its accuracy obvious to anyone with a mood disorder, and yet it's also counterintuitive to ordinary experience. If the self is illusory, how is it that we wake daily to the visceral presence of something as tenacious as an individual personality? Almost every morning—the instant my feet touch the floor—I immediately get that jolt of familiar dread. It's been waiting for me, and it plays havoc with the rest of the day, often leading to absurdity. I've snapped a toothbrush while brushing because my system's been that pumped with cortisol.

Ordinary objects can have an aura of menace. Usually I was the first to arrive, and also the first to leave the teacher's basement apartment, its windows decorated with Tibetan prayer flags. Placing my shoes in the same place each week felt stupidly important. Necessary. (Each time when I set down my shoes, the same memory arrives, showing the cluttered array of colourful boots, many having metal clasps, on the black mat by the door in grade one.) But when I (politely) hurried to depart before the others in the meditation class, seeing their footwear spread from the doorway into the kitchen made me uneasy. I don't know why, but the erratic crowd of mute winter boots and runners urged me to escape.

*

By coincidence, when I started the course, I'd been reading Fanny Howe's *The Needle's Eye*, her study of young people—from St. Francis to the Boston Marathon bombers—and came upon this observation about the ego from Simone Weil: "The thing we believe to be our self is as ephemeral and automatic of external circumstances as the form of a sea wave." But what if it's the strongest and most self-reliant people who can dispense with the self, whereas those with fewer defenses have to clutch at whatever's available? People's egos are so vulnerable, our needs so stark.

I once overheard a conversation in a rehab centre involving two elderly men, one in a wheelchair and attached to an oxygen tank, the other his healthy visitor. Unable to do anything concrete, he attempted to ~~comfort~~ console the ill man by pronouncing: "You'll be in a medical journal. Oh yeah, you can depend on it. Your case will be written up." What the patient replied to his friend, who was readying to leave, was inaudible. What passed between them may as well have been a conversation between a pool table and a hammer.

*

A pair of red-breasted nuthatches had been boring a hole for a nest in a nearby tree, but I hadn't seen nor heard them for almost two weeks. I was concerned that something bad had happened. One night I woke near 4:00 a.m. and began worrying, wondering where they might be. And this apprehension led to my own obsessive, trivial concerns alongside the acidic taste of insomnia. Anxiety remains a kind of unsought, thin membrane between the self and what's outside, a good tin roof depending on the weather.

*

Yet another mirror: the patience belonging to a scholar, someone whose inquisitive mode of thought combines attentiveness with erudition. I have a friend, Philip Charrier, who studies Japanese avant-garde photography.[1] Over the past two years, Philip translated Nakahira Takuma's manifesto "Why an Illustrated Botanical Dictionary?" into English, read the attendant criticism, and then wrote an article about the author. His is a sensibility that invests years of study to create a form of knowledge

---

1   It felt strange to watch Andrzej Wajda's film *Korczak* because Philip resembles the actor, Wojciech Pszoniak, who plays the hero, Janusz Korczak. Korczak was a child psychologist who ran an orphanage in the Warsaw Ghetto. Recognized by the Nazis as a figure with an international reputation, he was offered freedom numerous times, but he refused to abandon the children in his care. As a kind of secular Bodhisattva, he died with them at Treblinka in 1942. Even though the dialogue was in Polish, the actor's intonation and facial features reminded me of the man I know. It seemed that it was my friend who was the courageous doctor. I'd turned to this movie because of Michal Glowinski's Holocaust memoir describing what it had meant to be a child in the ghetto. Glowinski writes of the movie's uncanny use of black-and-white film, which creates a "grayness with no boundaries" that recalled the actual ghetto for him: "Watching the film I could not believe my eyes. I was seeing that discolored color—in essence, the antithesis of color—in the very form in which it had imprinted itself in my memory decades earlier."

that annuls oblivion, a tool that steps back from the market and partisan politics, their shared delight in coercion, and their enthusiastic addiction to distraction + rancor + noise.

*

For fuck's sake, get a move on, dickhead. Asshole, Jesus, c'mon already.

*

In *The Bodhisattva's Brain*, Owen Flanagan investigates the Buddhist belief that there is no intrinsic, permanent self by asking:

> are character traits dispositions, tendencies to express reliably certain patterns of perception, feeling, thinking, and behavior, similar perhaps to my know-how for bike riding, which is not in me as an area of my brain is in me, but is a disposition in me that is activated by my bike?

I read this passage one morning before walking to work, thinking of how consciousness is ubiquitous, yet unique to everyone; it's as though consciousness is an impossible, necessary something that casts a shadow in the rain. And then, later that day, I discovered how you don't need to go far from your doorstep to have the ineluctably complicated world suddenly rise up and look straight at you once more.

*

What if the most accurate discursive response to subjective reality is the diary? Instead of recasting experience into an autonomous artistic form that evades change, such as a poem or photograph, the diary aligns itself with the ongoing accumulation of haphazard events. In a diary, nothing can be completed. Every time I start a new entry, I'm ambivalent: on the one hand, there's this unease because I can never include everything, can *never catch up* with what continues to happen; but on the other hand, writing sentences in a notebook provides solace and also a sense of minor rebellion against this century's omnipresent social media. Writing in a diary, there's no need to curate the self for others. Here is solitude tempted by infinite regress. When I open the book and ponder the pages to be filled, there's some joy—goofily reminiscent of seeing untouched snow in the very early morning—and also alarm: what will those unwritten pages eventually contain that will embody the sporadic fragments of the world as they come cascading towards this very moment, somehow arriving from the invisible and directionless future?

*

Regina, Saskatchewan: April 28, 2017

Got up early to read Flanagan on Buddhist psychology. As I took Jakob to school, he told me more about his imaginary town in the Atlantic and the recent great white shark sightings there. Attended a ½ day meeting. Walked around Wascana Lake, the eastern part that's rarely visited.

At one point on the trail, near the Science Centre, a cyclist stopped, having noticed my binoculars, and asked if I was interested in birds. He told me of a heron he'd just seen. I went to the place beneath a willow tree he'd mentioned, and there it was, a kind of heron I'd never encountered before. Entirely camouflaged, it would have escaped my notice if the cyclist hadn't alerted me to its presence. I always feel unsettled, even humbled, by contingency: if I'd paused longer at the marsh when I was looking at some American avocets (a pair who'd fortunately survived last week's unexpected snowstorm and sub-zero temperatures), or if the meeting this morning hadn't gone over schedule, I wouldn't have met the cyclist and so would have missed what my field guide informs me was a black-crowned night heron. What's really intriguing, though, is the unanswerable question of what had shaped the cyclist's life to make him the kind of closely observant person who takes in birds while off-road biking.

Near Pine Island, met F. He retired last year. Perhaps because he and I both like to take photographs, he nodded at my binoculars, mistook them for a camera, and asked if I was out taking pictures. No, I said, bird watching. People see what they're used to seeing, it seems.

*

The heron had beguiling, almost infrared eyes with black-black-black widened pupils that took in the very slight movement when I lifted the binoculars. The bird had a motionless, nearly blue beak, mostly grey plumage, and the self-assured presence of a solitary predator.

*

One of the pleasures of street photography is that you go looking for something without knowing what it is until it actually appears—and then form and content cohere instantly, by willed chance. With binoculars, too, you don't know what you'll encounter, though cameras and binoculars aren't alike at all. Binoculars are strange. If they offer the immediate, addictive joy of seeing something that's normally inaccessible, they obviously retain nothing of what you've seen. Binocular vision also engages the body more thoroughly than when one takes pictures because it's restricted to the physical movement of lifting the binoculars to one's eyes and then remaining still, often for minutes. But when you lower the binoculars, the perceptual barrier of distance returns instantly, ejecting you from the magnified world. By placing us concretely within ongoing time as we observe what's happening, binoculars don't allow for the creation (and collection) of images; neither can we gain possession over what's far away. If binoculars allow the inhuman world to move toward us, they also don't insert the self into the world the way a camera does (however negligibly in street photography or overtly in a selfie). Binoculars expose us to the world's manifold temporal discontinuities. It's as though we're encompassed within time and yet simultaneously excluded from it.

Scanning across the lake, looking for grebes, sometimes I feel as though I'm not really there at all. And this uncanny sensation increases when I repeat the simple childhood act of glancing through the wrong end of the binoculars: I suddenly gain a sense of the various, unrepeatable gradations of subjective oblivion that are always coeval with any act of looking. Photography is different; it gestures towards meaning—whether semiotic or documentary—whereas binoculars simply acknowledge what's indivisibly there. One can only look. Not save. And yet this isn't the whole story, either. Reality also seems to have an immanent dimension that waits in potential for a camera to grant it some provisional form, whether someone passes by and takes a picture or not, notices anything or not. The photograph at the beginning of this essay contains someone on a bicycle, and this cyclist grants a kind of aesthetic coherence to the temple's windows, windows that function as mirrors reflecting some trees, a flicker of framed nature that is only present when perceived from the sidewalk on the city street, not from inside the rooms of the temple.

*

It's worth being reminded how there are so very few sets of eyes operating in any given chunk of terrestrial space: from sky to marsh, amidst trees, wind, mud, and across remodeled buildings with straying windows and the inevitable invisibly deteriorating staircases—amongst all these things and more—almost nothing is capable of seeing anything else.

*

I don't know how my friend who mistook my binoculars for a camera reacted to his perceptual error, or if he thought about it at all. We decide daily whether we'll allow our small slippages to unsettle us. If people can easily ignore reminders of how attentiveness to external reality fluctuates, what of interiority, the ways in which we connect to ourselves?

More than twenty years ago, I applied for a job at a university and, as it happened, gave a paper at a conference that someone on the department's search committee also attended. He didn't know me, and I chose not to introduce myself when we stood in an elevator together. A few years later, after we'd become colleagues, we had an occasion to discuss the past and he said to me: "Didn't we meet at that conference in Florida during the '90s? Yes, I remember meeting you at a panel." Saying this, his face lit up and I could see that, yes, indeed, he'd just remembered our initial meeting that had never happened. Somewhere in his brain a vivid image that was entirely erroneous had just been created, and I could tell that he could actually see it. That memory shifts is a commonplace, but it's quite another thing to witness this change the moment it takes place inside another person. I didn't disabuse him of his fabricated memory, but wondered how much human activity is engaged, consciously or not, with the continuous, largely imperceptible, dissolution of the continuous self. I don't believe I make these kinds of errors, but I must, and like everyone else perpetually rewrite my past. How can one take notice of these things? That we aren't in turmoil over this mental erosion rivets us to our carelessness as we move precariously along and within oblivion. We each pretend to know that it's our duty eventually to go missing, and yet, before then, deeply lost within our sense of the present, parts of us are chips of paint peeling off a fence near a factory a continent away from where we actually live.

My seven-year-old son Jakob is beginning to get interested in birds. One day after I saw the night heron, just after we'd participated in a demonstration protesting government inaction on global warming, I took him to the willow tree with our arthritic dog, and along with us was a guest visiting from British Columbia. I hoped we'd find the heron, but knew he might have already left to go further north. The visitor who was accompanying us (I'll say his name is David) is my mother-in-law's sort-of partner—since both he and she have OCD, their relationship is intricate, carefully scripted, though often erratic. Dave's addicted to Facebook, which given his age (he's 70) slightly surprised me, but shouldn't have: it's a perfect blend of entertainment and analgesic. He'd been taking dozens of pictures to post on his Facebook page, so I knew he'd want to take a photo of the heron if we managed to find it.

The bird was perched on a branch over the lake.

Dave took out his phone and I asked him not to get too close, but he did, and this meant he got several shots of a heron in full flight.

*

In her study on internet trolling, *This Is Why We Can't Have Nice Things*, Whitney Phillips observes:

> Facebook's basic architecture… positions the user as the subject of every sentence he or she utters, indeed as the center of his or her particular social universe. Self-involvement, in other words, is built into the code; one is primed to take things personally. This is not to say that Facebook users are solipsistic, exactly. But the relationship between user and content is, and is designed to be, solipsistic.

*

I mention these details because I've been reading *Essays in Idleness*, written by Kenkō, a Zen monk who lived during the Japanese medieval period, and he castigates people "who take all pleasures grossly," adding that "they get down and step on the snow, leaving footmarks, there is nothing that they do not regard as their own." This final remark clarified something I've been pondering since travelling several years ago to Auschwitz-Birkenau, where I noticed some visitors had inexplicably carved their initials into the barracks at Birkenau; earlier that year, I'd seen something similar when my family had been hiking in the Rockies. I was carrying Jakob in a backpack then, and we were walking along a mountain stream that unexpectedly opened up into a vista that showed an amazing (though doomed) glacier. This whole scene was desecrated by people who'd spray-painted their names on some boulders. And I didn't understand why people do such things until I read Kenkō and saw Dave maraud his way toward the bird on the shore of the lake: if people see what they think they see (as my friend mistook my binoculars for a camera), we also seem to believe that what we see belongs to us.

*

Dave's parents survived the Holocaust, and he hoards movies. They take up almost all of the space in his apartment. I've never been there—almost no one has—but apparently there's only a narrow pathway between the couch where he sleeps and the bathroom and kitchen, though he hasn't cooked in years. In fact, his kitchen cabinets are filled with movies. He lives on pizza that he can order in. Once, when he thought that his landlord was going to inspect his apartment for roaches, he threw over three hundred movies away in a dumpster, but then gave up: there were too many. Shortly after, he brought us two suitcases crammed full of VHS cassettes and DVDs, though he still owns thousands. A generous man with eclectic tastes, he once gave us Fassbinder's *Berlin Alexanderplatz* and Michael Powell's *Peeping Tom* to say thanks for our hospitality. But his memory is bad. When we talk about things that occurred during previous visits, I can tell that he doesn't remember them. Though he does recall that last year, upon learning I'd been reading about the Holocaust, he phoned his mother so he could introduce us. I was nervous to meet her this way, worrying that talking to a stranger out of the blue would be disturbing. But it wasn't; she quite openly told me of her experiences at Drancy, an internment camp outside Paris I'd only read about, having picked up a remaindered copy of Hélène Berr's diary. After a while, though, she'd had enough, and I gave the phone over to Dave and they spoke about his recent trip with his retired brother to Mexico.

*

As a child, the world around me insisted that the twentieth century was entirely, uniquely, special. From *Life* magazine to TV specials to the grownups surrounding me—from the alcoholic World War II veteran who taught music at the high school where my Dad was a geography teacher to the blonde Beatles fan who babysat me and my sister when my parents went to Montreal's Expo 1967—everyone in the know had no doubts that those of us living in the twentieth century were participating in the most exciting, most important, most unprecedented period in human history. (Still, I was too young to participate; it was as though everyone my age had missed what mattered and could never catch up. When postmodern theorists spoke about belatedness during the 1980s, I knew precisely what they meant.) But then I began to see pictures from the 1940s and to learn of the Nazis and Hiroshima, and the twentieth century as something exciting took on a darker dimension that I've never been able to understand. Something that started in my childhood and has continually perplexed me is the problem of simultaneity: what did it mean that I could sit in a cool basement during summer holidays in Canada and thumb through magazines showing mutilated children and soldiers in faraway Vietnam? This simple but unequal equation has never left me. How could it be that when Anne Frank was sent to Auschwitz in 1944, my parents were five-year-old kids living safely in small-town southern Ontario?

Simultaneity is utterly bewildering.

On November 30, 1943, before she was sent to Drancy, Berr (only twenty-three) wrote: "The only immortality of which we can have certain knowledge is the immortality that consists in the continuing memory of the dead among the living." Unknown to her, Etty Hillesum, a Dutch diarist and writer sometimes called the "adult counterpart to Anne Frank," died at Auschwitz-Birkenau that day (only twenty-nine), somehow a Tuesday for both women: *mardi*: *dinsdag*. A few days later in early December, 1943, Berr wrote that she could "dance, run and skip" because a woman she knew had received a postcard from her daughter at Birkenau that had been posted several weeks before. Berr was in France: she could have had no idea as to what that meant, though she eventually would: like Anne Frank, she and her family were deported to Auschwitz, and like the fifteen-year-old, she died at Bergen-Belsen only days before the camp was liberated.

Diaries. When I mentioned earlier that starting a new diary gives me a sense of trepidation because of not knowing what its unwritten pages might eventually contain, I was repressing something much grimmer: neither Hélène Berr, Etty Hillesum, nor Anne Frank knew whether an entry would become the final one because each day was uncertain. For each diarist a moment came when she could no longer write because of being deported to Poland, a place of rumour and uncertainty until the selection took place upon their arrival at Birkenau.

*

As I write these words, a recently migrated Swainson's Thrush is scavenging around the garden near the old sink my wife has turned into a fountain, and Dave has been making plans on the Internet to vacation with his brother in the Galapagos Islands next year.

*

As I consider Dave's family history, associative thought immediately makes me realize with a sick thud that there's something worsening with my memory. When I wrote in my diary (on April 28) about the cyclist and his gift, I entirely forgot about a much more jarring instance of contingency that had happened only a few days before the cyclist took a moment to speak with me. I'd attended an annual Holocaust memorial service with Dave and my mother-in-law at the local synagogue (commemorating the anniversary of the Warsaw Ghetto uprising in April 1943).[2] I go to this service most years, and it usually features a survivor.

This time, upon entering the synagogue, I noticed an acquaintance who's recently developed an interest in Judaism. This person is fluidly gendered and was wearing one of the black kippahs the synagogue keeps on hand. Before the service began, the rabbi seemed distracted, and then he told us that the invited guest, Amek Adler, had died that morning in a hospital downtown.

*

Adler had lived 89 years, and the previous night he'd spoken to students in Humbolt, Saskatchewan. He'd been born in Lublin, Poland, moved to Łódź with his family as a boy, was sent to the Warsaw Ghetto, somehow avoided Treblinka, and was eventually deported to Auschwitz before being liberated in Dachau in 1945. Between then and now, he'd

---

2   Neither Berr nor Hillesum mention the Warsaw Uprising in their writing; it's highly likely that they were ignorant of what was happening in Poland during the spring of 1943.

married a woman who'd been sent on a *Kindertransport* to Stockholm, and they'd made their way to Toronto during the 1950s. And this man ultimately died in Regina, Saskatchewan, on a Tuesday morning in the early twenty-first century, closing an immeasurable vacuum that keeps widening—

*

When I began this essay I hadn't intended it to move toward violence. Because it seemed a happy accident that I'd read Flanagan referring to the somatic memory of riding a bicycle the same day I'd met the cyclist who pointed out the heron, I'd wanted to approach the Buddhist critique of the permanent self through the lens of contingency. But thinking about Adler's recent death breaks everything apart.

What does it mean to conceive of the Holocaust in the twenty-first century? What claims does it still exert on us? I don't know how to respond, though I feel it's necessary to try including what the Holocaust contains when pondering human experience. When one considers evil, human possibility, chance, and the durability of the self under horrendous conditions, the Holocaust exists as a kind of relentless limit case for all thought.[3] But I don't have the courage to open myself to what the Holocaust holds. I need continual reminders to jar me into rethinking it. And in all of this, I feel a kind of involuntary despondency, entirely unearned through personal grief, a despondency that persists all the same. I'm not Jewish, but my wife and our son are; her ancestors immigrated to Canada from Poland in the early twentieth century. How can one possibly understand the implications of that decision?

---

3   It is an open question whether the Holocaust has been relegated to being perceived generally as a past event characterizing the worst of the twentieth century, rather than an ongoing problem and crisis that refuses to be resolved. This essay cannot sketch out the intricacies of this issue, though I will point out two approaches that acknowledge the necessity of regarding the Holocaust as something that intrudes upon contemporary experience: in *Radical Evil*, Richard J. Bernstein evaluates ethical theory—from Kant to Levinas—by challenging it to account for Auschwitz; Ben Taub, describing the plight of sub-Saharan refugees in their attempts to reach Europe, refers to how "the German embassy in Niger sent a cable to Berlin… comparing the conditions in Libya's migrant connection houses to those of Nazi concentration camps. Sometimes the sick are buried alive." Both writers imply that the Holocaust indicts our seemingly endless capacity for indifference to the pain of others. What would it mean to be the civil servant who read this cable in Berlin and then looked south out of a window in the Reichstag in the direction of Paul Eisenman's Memorial to the Murdered Jews of Europe a few streets away?

One can make donations and political gestures, but what does it mean to ponder violence and suffering? These questions seem obligatory yet futile, and their futility necessarily stalls us midstream. It's as though one moment we're freely conversing in our native tongue and the next, the language has unaccountably changed and we can only discern a few words in this foreign speech, and then, right after that, we're suddenly surrounded by a palpable, immediate silence in which we can neither hear nor say anything.

*

Does juxtaposition—whether it's formal in an artwork or random in actual life—create something new, or is it arbitrary, something merely cast about by the wind, a plastic grocery bag caught in a tree or a tern buffeted above a lake detecting a fish beneath the water's surface?

*

My son loves to draw animals—these days it's mostly sharks—but a little while ago he drew what was quite clearly a grey cockatiel. I asked him about it and he told me it was "Echo," which meant nothing to me. This confused him, so he reminded me that two summers ago we'd bird-sat Echo (named for his skills at mimicry) for a few weeks. It took me several seconds to push through the nothingness in my mind, sequestering me there, until I could find the barest glimpse of the bird. My capacity for short-term memory seems to have atrophied. It hasn't always been like this: I first read Kafka's *The Metamorphosis* when I was twenty, and rereading it decades later, I found myself remembering what would occur on the next page. It's difficult not to panic: I don't know what is happening, and I'm at a loss as to what to do.

*

I hesitate to emphasize personal experience in an essay that mentions the Holocaust. But how can one ever avoid the way subjectivity colours perception and thought? After years of worsening short-term memory problems and bouts of insomnia that psychiatrists and counselors were unable to resolve, I finally visited a neuropsychologist who gave me an extensive series of tests that resulted in a diagnosis of NLD (nonverbal learning disability, though now it's called NVLD), something he explained to me as being "a developmentally-based disorder that is often associated with deficits in nonverbal communication and perception." People with NVLD find technology intimidating, experience acute anxiety and inexplicable mood shifts, and find it hard to "adjust" to social difficulties. Reading another person's facial cues is problematic. Given to obsession, we also consider our immediate environments to be intrinsically threatening. Apparently, we usually retreat into solitude and are susceptible to depression. (The news that my chronic depression is likely the result of the learning disability was astonishing.) People with NVLD are also prone to substance abuse. Apparently, I've had this condition all my life, and have "historically compensated" for these weaknesses by relying on verbal skills and developing a keen memory. Learning to use words became a form of psychic survival.

But my words are disappearing. I keep a notebook filled with words I encounter that I know I've not used in years. *Probity, auspicious, exasperate*. After I had an MRI, the neurologist showed me pictures of my brain filled with dark threads. Decades of anxiety and substance abuse have possibly caused this damage. It might plateau, the doctor said. Will words continue to be scoured away from my neurons? How can I prepare for this inevitability?

*

Almost every time I drop Jakob off at school, he refuses to play with his friends until I'm entirely out of sight. He stands by the fence at the edge of the school property waving good-bye, and I'm reminded of how parents were forced to be separated from their children so that they could be sent into the unknown on *Kindertransport*. I'm ashamed of this sort of thinking because I know my son spends the day nearby, and this emotion blurs with pity for the parents back in Europe during the 1930s. This shame has the metallic taste insomnia does, and I wonder whether my son will inherit my psychic genes… I fear he may also be attracted to self-destructive behavior. If so, meditation helps, I'll tell him; meds too, and reading; exercise eventually, but what's most important is to recognize the long, slow pair of eyes inside that's been watching everything from almost the very beginning, when your consciousness started to determine where it is and what it's for. Seems to be for.

*

Once, in my twenties, I was sitting in the Art Gallery of Ontario's cafeteria when I suddenly felt that I was being watched. Not by anyone in the room, but by something from within. It was as though what constituted my "self" was afloat on water, and way down beneath, there was an entity observing "me." It was neither hostile nor affable, though it did emanate power. And it seemed older than I was, somehow; stronger too, and more astute. I sensed it was judging me, but that didn't seem to be its central task. Perhaps it had no purpose at all. It was there, it looked, and I knew that whatever took place on the water, on the surface, what my life actually was—living with my high-school girlfriend, visiting Toronto for the weekend, working nights stocking shelves in a grocery store—none of this meant anything to it. *I* was insignificant. My life was transparent to what those eyes saw, and for this reason I've called it "the watcher," which isn't right; the word sounds too much like some totemic spirit in a fantasy novel.

In her diary, Hillesum writes that, after waking up from a nap, she noticed "that there is some substance, or whatever you like to call it, inside one, something that leads a life of its own." I can't say whether what she observed is her version of what I felt or something different. I note, though, that she became aware of this interior substance after a nap. Waking up not in the morning, but after a nap, feels different to me, too; it takes several minutes to adjust to the solidity of daily life. Perhaps wandering around paintings shifts attention away from ordinary immediacy in such a way that some form of alien interiority can be glimpsed—except that it's not that tidy. That moment in the cafeteria when I was twenty-one was the only time I'd been aware of those eyes.

Until last week, when they appeared once again.

I hesitate to lay words over the experience because they might obscure it. There were the eyes again, after several decades. I instantly recognized their gaze, but the entity was different. It took me a moment to determine what had changed: the gaze seemed tired, so bone tired not even a belt of tequila would rouse or revive whatever this force is. And then I understood. That substance that Hillesum says leads a life of its own had seemingly lost something of the autonomy it had before, and its intensity was much less than I remembered. It had aged. This seemed impossible. I'd always thought of it as outside of time, circumstance, change of any sort. But this aging had weakened it, made it seem brittle: something had made it suffer, but from *what* I can't discern. The sensation lasted only seconds. Will I ever encounter it again, and if so, what sort of condition will we both be in? What concerns me is that the gaze seemed stiffer, less energetic, and it seemed to have turned inward so that it was paying attention to itself, not the world. For a moment I wondered whether it had become lonely. I don't know what triggered its unexpected arrival, but I don't think it's a coincidence that this recent appearance also took place in an art gallery. Art points to things in us we've missed, somehow confirms that we live many lives inside, and not all of them at the same speed. Back when I first realized I was being observed, had in fact been observed all of my life, I'd been in Toronto for a Van Gogh exhibition, and earlier that morning I'd bought a newspaper that contained an interview with a cantankerous Lech Wałęsa, who had only just galvanized the Solidarity Movement in Gdańsk. When I saw this interior gaze again, I was taking in some black-light paintings and an adroit neon installation in a local art gallery down the street from my home in Regina.

*

There seem to be numerous voices inside the psyche, not only eyes. When I was diagnosed with depression, my first wife Lynn and I were living in a Toronto apartment above a health-food store.[4] I'd been prescribed Prozac. One morning, several weeks into taking the drug, I was out on the balcony, having the morning's first cigarette. A TTC bus went by, and something flashed inside my head. After weeks of nothing, the Prozac took effect, not gradually but immediately. An entirely unfamiliar feeling of well-being suddenly filled me, but something else accompanied the sensation. In that instant I realised that I wasn't alone. *Welcome back*—two words spoken clearly from what felt like the back of my mind. But it wasn't a single, elated voice; I recognized that it was speaking on behalf of several others. And all of them knew me.

I know that I'm mentally ill, but I don't think I'm psychotic. The voice was absolutely real; it was also utterly distinct from me, the person I always woke up inside each morning. And I knew that the

---

4   Because of the store, our apartment was busy with cockroaches. Our first child, Andy, was born a year later, and it's possible that their asthma results from being exposed to cockroaches and disinfectants when they were a baby.

voice was right; it *was* precisely as though I'd returned to where I was supposed to be. Of course, up until then, I'd no idea I'd been off somewhere, lost and missing, not living the life I was supposed to live. I suppose an obvious question would be: was the voice that greeted me linked to the eyes that I mentioned earlier? Had that observer decided to communicate with words? No. The two sensations were completely different. I don't know enough about psychology to identify the nature of these alien but non-threatening presences, but I can say the voice left me with a sense of relief. Instead of shitty, I felt clean, even vigorous. Stable. But no medication has ever worked for long, and I've never heard that chorus again. And I don't know if I'm living the life today that I'm supposed to live or whether I've gone completely astray again.

*

The nuthatches remain missing.

*

Days can be lived objects that are incommensurate with themselves. One afternoon I receive an email from a friend who tells me that her husband has been diagnosed with the early stages of Alzheimer's, and then at dusk that evening, Jakob and I go to the Science Centre where a biologist is releasing some brown bats who were rescued over the winter and kept indoors in a display until this spring. These bats have day-glow strips placed on them so the people gathered can see them fly off into the woods upon their release. The strips will fall off in the next day, but when each bat begins its uncertain flight across a small field in the near dark and then makes its way to the woodlands, a crowd of excited children can see where it's headed and boisterously chase after it.

*

Łódź as associative thought. In *The Emigrants*, W.G. Sebald notes that Łódź was once "known as *polski Manczester*" because both cities embodied early industrialization. Today, Sunday, June 4, 2017, people in Manchester are keeping their brand-new tattoos clean, tattoos showing the simple outline of a bee, the Mancunian bee, symbol of the city's dedication to hard work, a symbol that's persisted since the nineteenth century. Many of these people with new tattoos possibly attended the memorial concert Ariana Grande performed in Manchester six hours ago in tribute to the victims of the suicide bombing that took place in the city thirteen days ago. The bomber killed and wounded mostly women and young girls.

The bee's original significance has now been irrevocably changed because the tattoos are being worn in solidarity with all these people, those who are gone and their fellow citizens who remain. Each in need of being seen, each in need of protection.

WHEN A GLACIER BREATHES, JOHANNES, IT RELEASES RAVENS

Fragments are the only form I trust…. See the moon? It hates us.
—Donald Barthelme, "See the Moon?"

It wasn't until my early 50s that I was diagnosed with a learning disability. Until I learned of it much of my life was awry: simply inexplicable. And yet, despite my now having an awareness of the problem, anxiety continues to blossom like algae.

Prozac helped with my mood disorders for a while. Ditto Paxil. Pristiq, ah, *no.* Trintellix; and Siv-Mirtazapine, we'll see.

My drug of choice used to be beer, followed by red wine, then tequila. Always nicotine. For fun in my teens and early twenties: LSD, weed, magic mushrooms, scoops of bennies.

When I recently discovered that a psychologist who engages in pioneering research in NVLD believes that, of those who have learning disabilities, it is those with NVLD who are most prone to suicide, I wonder about psychic autonomy. Seen one way, there's almost nothing that's more expressive of the individual subjective will than when someone freely rejects what their life has entailed and chooses to end it. And yet, how can anyone who's ever been diagnosed with a chronic mental disability not be undermined by the fact that what previously felt like autonomy has likely been profoundly compromised by something of which they weren't aware before diagnosis?

I have boxes of diaries going back to adolescence, most written with fountain pen, and in one of them I taped the blade from a case cutter left over from grocery-store shifts after I used it to slice up my left arm, legs, and shoulders because I didn't have the guts to go further.

A feeling of failure so corrosive it requires a soundtrack containing a trio of dead men, each playing an accordion.

Are Lauren Berlant and Kathleen Stewart right to claim that personality is scar tissue?

*

When I look into an interior mirror, these are some of the reflections I see:

—My first memory seems to be the assassination of JFK: all I can remember is a TV screen in my grandparents' living room, some KFC, and the feeling that something was off-kilter. The adults in my life were upset in an unusual way. Upon her death from diabetes three years later, my beloved grandmother gave me the permanent gift of knowing that reality is partially woven from the sense that something is utterly wrong.

—A neighbour alerted my mother when she found three of my GI Joes crucified on crosses I made from sawed hockey sticks, which I left in the woods behind our house when I was a boy. Red magic marker made their hands and feet look bloody.

—Walking alongside an enormous indoor cage that held a tiger, it following me. The zoo in Detroit was dilapidated, and I'd never been watched by an animal that intently. "He wants to eat you," my mother said, but I can't see her in the memory. It's damp, cooler than outside. I know the tiger can't get out of the cage. I can also sense that there's something ancient inside the tiger; it is much older than its actual age. It's older than any animal I'll ever encounter, this creature following me in grimy sunlight on the wet cement floor.

—Trees in a campground outside Munich. The German campers are all wearing Adidas track suits, which is very strange to our Canadian eyes. Back home, only athletes wear track suits. I can smell pine. It's July 19, 1972. I'm looking at pictures in a guidebook my Dad bought at Dachau concentration camp only a few hours before.

In a recent study on Holocaust diaries, Amos Goldberg observes that "for significant numbers of non-Jews the Holocaust acts as a central identity-founding event." He doesn't probe this odd situation, though I wish he did. When my parents took our family to Dachau when I was twelve, neither they nor I grasped that the visit would permeate my unconscious, eventually resulting in a life-long obsession with the death camps.[5] Whatever it was that affected me that July afternoon went underground for decades. While I can't say for certain when thoughts of the Holocaust began to return persistently, I remember holding Andy only hours after their birth by C-section in 1996. Lynn was asleep—her difficult labour had gone from 10:00 p.m. on a Tuesday night until sometime after 6:00 p.m. the next day—and I, too, was exhausted. As I held our first child, I felt two things: nothing anywhere was as important as they were; and then immediately something else—other parents must feel the same way, but those who had to protect children during the Yugoslavian war that was currently taking place, or earlier, those who had waited their turns for the gas chambers at Auschwitz-Birkenau, these parents hadn't the luxury of holding a sleeping child safely in a downtown Toronto hospital.

*

When the three of us moved from our apartment above the health food store in Toronto to Regina, we rented in a townhouse complex. There was a bit of sidewalk and grass between the rows of homes like a U. Among our neighbours was single mother who worked at a car rental service. She had two boys; the youngest used to squash grasshoppers

---

5   It concerns me that this desire to educate myself about the Holocaust may have a psychological origin, rather than being an honest attempt to recognize what happened, to respond to the claim it has upon us. Christopher Bollas argues that individuals may seek out aesthetic moments that entail "an uncanny fusion with the [transformational] object, an event that prevailed during early psychic life. However, such occasions, meaningful as they are, are less noteworthy as transformational accomplishments than they are for their uncanny quality, the sense of being reminded of something never cognitively comprehended but existentially known…. It is well to remember that an individual may seek a negative aesthetic experience, for such an occasion 'prints' his early ego experiences and registers the structure of the unknown thought. Some borderline patients, for example, repeat traumatic situations because through the latter they remember their origins existentially."

between thumb and forefinger and say, "I'll crush your nipples." His brother would knock on our door, asking for food. They would be men now. When Lynn and I unpacked in Regina we found only one stow-away cockroach in the boxes. I haven't seen one since.

*

Much of my professional life has involved teaching and writing about the short story. A question recurs in class discussions, one posed by A.S. Byatt in her review of Alice Munro's *The Love of a Good Woman*: "Do we experience life as a continuum or as a series of disconnected shocks and accidents?" Both positions are accurate enough, though the depressive in me knows that I'm continuously fastened to events in the past that took me by surprise, and that events such as these can sever a life from itself. And then there are those appalling moods that one continually orbits, psychic centres of gravity that can be predicted as often as they can be triggered by unforeseen constellations of events, accidental conversations, or the look in another's eyes when they're angry.

Another question the short story revolves around concerns ethical and psychological hermeneutics. In *The Genesis of Secrecy*, Frank Kermode sympathetically refers to Wilhelm Dilthey's notion of the "impression-point," that incisive moment of a life or a text which "gives articulation to the whole." James Joyce's Gabriel Conroy experiences a psychological impression-point when he grasps that he needs finally to permit finitude to enter his life as he watches Greta asleep in their hotel room while snow falls in Dublin.[6] Thinking of an impression-point in ethical terms perplexes our civilization. It doesn't know how to resolve whether an action (or series of related actions) defines a life. Consider Kaing Guek Eav (Comrade Duch), once a math teacher in Cambodia, who eventually commanded S–21, a detention centre run by the Khmer Rouge in Phnom Penh during the late 1970s. According to Michael Paterniti, Duch had initially overseen "a jungle prison camp, where he'd studiously refined his ideas about torture, and was then put in charge of S–21… [where] he condoned 'living autopsies.'" Later in life, Duch converted to Christianity and worked as a health supervisor for refugees.

---

6   Part of the psychic whole that infuses Gabriel's self-understanding (and the epiphany in Joyce's "The Dead") is that he's ignorant of contingency: it is only by chance that Greta is reminded of her teenage love. It is an open question whether Gabriel will be able to throw off the weight of his relentless self-absorption when he and his wife wake the next morning to a snowy Dublin.

Ultimately placed on trial for crimes against humanity in 2009, he was sentenced to serve nineteen years in prison. Observing Duch's remorse at the trial and the way he "devoted his full attention to each witness" who testified against him, the philosopher Alphonso Lingis asks: "what would be accomplished, for him and for us, and for twelve thousand people now dead, by imprisoning him for the rest of his life?"

Comrade Duch died on September 2, 2020, of a lung disease. His body had no autopsy because it was immediately cremated owing to concerns about COVID.

*

Put yourself in another's agitated shoes, honesty being not so much a pursuit as a performance requiring its own diagnosis.

*

[The essay] thinks in fragments, just as reality itself is fragmentary, and finds its unity in and through the breaks and not by glossing them over…. Discontinuity is essential to the essay…. The essay has to cause the totality to be illuminated in the partial feature, whether the feature be chosen or merely happened upon, without asserting the presence of the totality.
—Theodor W. Adorno, "The Essay as Form"

*

When I write a poem, I always implicitly address it to Don Coles, something I did when he was alive and still do now that he's gone. I studied with him in my early twenties, as did Lynn, and we invited him to our wedding. He wasn't able to attend, but he gave us a collection of essays by Robert Hass and book of poems by Geoffrey Hill as a wedding present. The Hass volume is with me, the Hill, Lynn. Although we wrote to congratulate him when he won the Governor General's Award in 1993, we gradually lost touch, and twenty years passed between the final class I took with him at York University and when I met him for lunch at his favourite restaurant in Toronto, Grano's, in 2006. I was in Toronto to launch my first book, a collection of short stories.

As we looked at the menu, he tried to summon up the particular group of students who made up our class so long before, and I reminded him of a reading he'd done when he published *Landslides*. The title poem describes visiting his mother at the Gericare Centre in Woodstock, where she was suffering from Alzheimer's. To this day, I can recall when he read of wet, yellow leaves on asphalt, leaves he'd seen on a particular visit with his mother when she still had a sense of what was happening to her. Had she died then, Don wrote, while she could still demonstrate a degree of awareness, he wouldn't have begun the poem. But she continued to deteriorate. Her misery caused Don to understand what he calls "the intimate cynicism of the world." As he read of the autumn leaves in the rain that late afternoon in the 1980s, my memory pulled in such colours summoned by rain, a paved driveway, the safety in childhood of returning from the library with books on a day in October. And as he continued to read, the line identifying the world's intimate cynicism slammed into me from nowhere. If I can't quite hear his voice today, I can still picture the image in my mind that his words created: it had such tender, brutal beauty. At the end of the reading, during the question period, I asked whether he would read that specific section again, the one with the yellow leaves—and he did. But there at Grano's some twenty years later, he easily remembered the reading because he recalled a young asshole who asked him to reread a section from the poem. I don't remember his name, he said. The bastard, he went on, he could tell that I almost lost control when I read the section the first time and he wanted to see if I'd crack. But I didn't, Don told me. I read it again, and I didn't stumble.

*

Don and I met at Grano's every time I visited Toronto. I revelled in his lovely habit of turning his body sideways when he laughed. Even today, I can see him telling me that the light in Bergman's films is devoid of anything that could bring harm into the world... when we both get brain freeze. What's the name of Bergman's central male actor?

*

These fragments—written in a kind of abbreviated code—can't avoid being incoherent even when they're their most precise.

*

Max von Sydow: 1929-2020   Anne Frank: 1929-45

When I aim to get my 200 minutes a week of hard cardio on a second-hand stationary bike in the sunroom here upstairs… overlooking two well-stocked bird feeders, I listen to Nine Inch Nails to provide inspirational anger. Nirvana: energy. Self-pity: Joy Division. Strenuous exercise at my age teaches decay.

Why didn't anyone tell Joy Division that it was wrong to choose the band's name because they thought that's what the Nazis called the sex slaves they kept in camp bordellos?

Is anything innocent?

I once drove to Butte, Montana, because I wanted to see whether the town really had the amazing colours Wim Wenders gives it in his movie *Don't Come Knocking*.

*

I've never felt at home anywhere but, if given a choice, would live in Amsterdam.

*

My favourite painters are Rembrandt, Vermeer, and Rothko. Always Anselm Kiefer. Gerhard Richter.

And also what the water gave Frida Kahlo.

*

Reading *The Shock of the Anthropocene*, I have at long last realised that historical knowledge is as important as philosophy for apprehending the present and its various manifestations of reality. There is an invisible Model-T Ford parked beneath the bird feeders swaying in the wind and snow. But beneath the Model T is something else. Oil's insatiable fire on the sunflower seeds and worn-down snow. And what is oil? In her study *Living Oil: Petroleum Culture in the American Century*, Stephanie LeMenager is blunt: "Oil was literally conceived of as a replacement for slave labour."

Could someone please do a cost-benefit analysis of what it means to be alive now?

*

When I was a child, my parents often had parties on Saturday nights. After a dance at the community centre, they once convinced the band to come home and play in the furnished basement where Dad had built his own bar, using cedar shakes for decoration. On Sunday mornings before church, while my Mom and Dad were still asleep, my sisters and I would explore the clutter in the basement, sometimes nibbling a bit of cold pizza from the beer fridge, always helping ourselves to leftover chips and pretzels, the strange dip my mother used to make for parties out of sour cream and a dried soup mix with small noodles and spices.

Secrets spilled from the upholstery like leaking bags of sleeping and hungover grownups, their brilliant hours having vanished into perfunctory place-holders: it's a pity that time was an undeterred hoax that eventually maimed them. My father has always believed an invisible dome would keep him—but not my mother, no—tolerably safe all the days he stays inside his dreams of being an exception.

And the gathering
Graces would come by Sunday mornings to

collect ashtrays and a few glasses of old scotch, an elixir that smells of golden burlap and some kind of music that's kept underground and to
repudiate the colour slide show of car crashes, heart attacks

and what keeps getting abandoned
like old swimwear in the mind—

*

The intimate cynicism of the world.

*

A hummingbird makes a Rothko of air—

*

36

Working as a steward in a private businessman's club when I was twenty-two—no women, not even a female letter carrier, were ever allowed through the door—taught me lickety-split that Karl Marx had fully understood the nature of his foe.

*

Once I was in a banquet hall for a conference in Lisbon and listened to Amari Baraka give an impromptu speech chastising a well-known literary theorist sitting two tables away, a man who emphasized epistemology in his books over history, politics, and race. The latter left midway through the jeremiad; afterwards there was a small amount of applause, but mostly silence.

How attentive should a person be to the events, ideas, and debates of their time?

—the reader might listen to "Fitter, Happier" by Radiohead from *OK Computer*

—the reader might further identify something significant that took place last year, and then try clarifying what shape it will take next Monday, and then scrutinise what happens to it when History does what it does, taking apart and reassembling everything that ↔ has come before.

*

Skyrim: the video game that currently obsesses Jakob, who could be mistaken for a Viking (though ½ of his heritage is Ashkenazi).

*

Though my model for this form comes from Susan Sontag, Fanny Howe, and David Markson, it seems that writing in fragments has very much become a contemporary style: Maggie Nelson, Jenny Offill, and Patricia Lockwood are practitioners who come to mind. I'm unsure what lies behind their choices to write in this mode, but mine is derived from an abiding interest in what constitutes a detail. Ezra Pound's "A Station in the Metro": a still photograph.

A resonant detail is something in the world beyond the self, something that looks into you.

*

Expected or unexpected, the moment that exposes and disarms the sinister passage of time.
—Michel Leiris, *The Ribbon at Olympia's Throat*

Time can't be disarmed, but there are moments that embody its passage. Walking by a sex shop on Granville Street in Vancouver after having a sushi dinner with a friend I've known for almost three decades, I notice a piece of paper taped to the glass door from the inside: "Closed because of family emergency. SORRY!"

*

And: a fragment as conceptual art: "Wondering when and where the last casual street-corner conversation in Latin might have taken place," ponders David Markson.

*

Ignoring the news while Amy, Jakob, and I have been in Golden, British Columbia, mostly to go hiking (when there's no smoke from forest fires), I've only just learned that Charlie Watts, the drummer for the Rolling Stones, died three days ago. I saw the Stones twice when I was a teenager: once at Buffalo's Rich Stadium on their *Some Girls* tour in 1978 (72,000 fans); the second time at their benefit concert for the Canadian National Institute for the Blind (CNIB), part of the sentence ordered by a judge for Keith Richards' being busted for possession just days before the band partied with our current prime minister's mother, Margaret Trudeau. I also learned this morning that the Liberals are trailing the Tories in the polls. Justin was seven when his mom hung out with the Stones; it was his parents' wedding anniversary. Today his younger brother and father are dead, and his mother is seventy-two. If connecting details can be a spurious pastime—Maggie Trudeau met the Stones on March 21, 1977, one week before Amy was born—these sorts of details very frequently embody what Leiris calls the "sinister passage of time."

"I wouldn't want my wife associatin' with us," drummer Charlie Watts grinned in 1977, as Margaret posed with the Stones in Toronto.

*

Fragments can be accumulated endlessly, though their arrival always takes me by surprise. This morning Jakob told me that he'd learned on the Internet that tigers will likely be extinct in thirty years. Only yesterday, I read the following sentences by Graham Harman, the founder of object-oriented ontology:

> Somewhere in his correspondence, H.P. Lovecraft makes the best case for embracing mortality that I have ever read: to the effect that, as we age, reality continues to change in ways increasingly uncomfortable to those of our generation, until finally a world arrives in which we would no longer care to live. For my own part, I have no wish to live into a future that witnesses the extinction of tigers and elephants.

*

When I read *Speak, Memory* by Vladmir Nabokov and later read his command—*Caress the detail, the divine detail*, I knew I had found the motto I could live by.
—Patricia Hampl, "The Dark Art of Description"

But what is a detail?

In literature, details can offer compression. From Alice Munro's "Passion": while Neil (the eventual suicide) sleeps, the central character Grace abandons him and goes to a river where she encounters a "sign warn[ing] that profanity, obscenity or vulgar language was forbidden in this place and would be punished." Anyone who has chafed at living in southern Ontario will recognize its tendency to tame reality through surveillance in these few words. An entire ethos is here.

(Additionally, the motive for Neil's suicide is nearly present in the sign's admonition.)

But details from actual life aren't so obviously sculpted: the dog on leash, a female boxer named Ruby, held her toy octopus tightly in her jaws as she accompanied her owner down the sidewalk on Main Street in Revelstoke, British Columbia, during the fire season of 2021. Flakes of ash fell through the air. After taking Ruby's picture, we drove to our motel, but first needed to turn the wipers on to clean the windshield.

En route to Vancouver from Calgary that day, we'd wanted to make it as far as Hope, but when we phoned ahead to secure lodging, we found that the motels were full, mostly with Trans Mountain Pipeline workers. The final one we called was booked equally with pipeline workers and fire fighters. What collects these various components into a detail is Ruby's octopus.

*

To Jan Zwicky, our sensitivity to details in the phenomenal world is primarily because we are creatures (among various others) capable of reading signs. And what we read in particular signs are gestalts: "Imagistic perception picks up on the force fields of gestalts that inform individual things... the whole is experienced through the particular, which is part of it." And suddenly perceiving a gestalt grants an unexpected joy. Moreover, to Zwicky, the capacity to respond to large and intricate gestalts is crucial if one is to place oneself within ecological networks.

The question arises whether such details exist objectively in the world or are transformed into moments of significance by the pattern-forming human mind. Amy and I were once hiking toward Edith Cavell glacier when we heard a loud crack sever something in the cold air above the glacier. What we heard was the glacier breaking. When I was a boy I was familiar with the sound of ice breaking in spring in the river that went through the town. This was utterly different: at Edith Cavell, it was if lightning spoke. Just then, a small girl came up to us, asking if we'd seen her parents. Both the glacier and the lost child were independent of me, and they seemed to be part of something large: the majesty and fragility of finite beings.[7]

Years later, in a poem dedicated to one of Vermeer's paintings, I wanted to offer the artist something back in gratitude for his work. It suddenly came to me that something I could extend in his direction, a man who had likely never seen a mountain, let alone a glacier, was this:

---

7   On the question of mind-independent reality and gestalts, Zwicky writes: "Since we and other beings demonstrate the capacity for accurate gestalt perception in a wide variety of situations, evolutionary theory suggests that such a capacity must be adaptive; if the capacity is adaptive, what it registers is real; ergo, gestalts must be mind-independent. At least they are as mind-independent as it gets. *How* mind-independent is mind-independent reality? No physicist or philosopher has been able to propose a fully satisfactory answer to this question... I propose to leave it open."

When a glacier breathes, Johannes, it releases ravens. When
a glacier breathes, earth grinds against the greyest sky, each

                                                     without

pain—
       They're morphine hiccups that split
time:

into a spray   of snow

*

But these details aren't fragments. They don't quite embody what
Friedrich Schlegel means when he outlines the autonomous nature of
the fragment: "A fragment, like a miniature work of art, has to be
entirely isolated from the surrounding world and be complete in itself
like a hedgehog." The black object on the right of this slab of concrete is a great blue heron; the other birds are pelagic cormorants. Off
in the distance, Stanley Park. Happening upon this construction by
the Vancouver waterfront, my friend Paul Endo and I both instantly
reached for our cameras, him first. (I met him when we both started
doctoral work in Toronto, he working on the sublime in Shelley and
Stevens, me on the short fiction of Donald Barthelme.) What makes
this image a fragment is the haphazard, randomly occurring red cloth
in the lower left of the shape, stationary, unlike the birds or the speed-
boat creating a spray in the upper right of the photograph. Nor to
forget the reflections, slightly rocking in almost nonexistent waves,
subject to change yet always obeying the same laws of physics as they
form and reform.

The American pelicans are going to disappear from the creek soon but should return in a few months before heading south for the winter. Their wingtips are the colour of the four crows chastising an unleashed dog in the park. A woman eating an ice cream cone just rode past on a bicycle. And then a father goes by explaining evolution to his youngest daughter, who's riding shotgun on his shoulders.
    —Diary notes: June 4, 2010

Dürer died from a fever he caught in a Dutch swamp, where he had gone to look at a stranded whale.
    —David Markson, *Wittgenstein's Mistress*

After years of renting a house in a rough neighbourhood in Regina, my second wife Amy and I finally bought a small house in one of the more beautiful areas of town. The new tenant of the place we once lived stayed only two months because she came home one evening to find a noose hanging from a beam in the basement. The worst that happened to us when we lived there was a broken passenger window on our old car (the car's owner's manual stolen—according to the police, likely an initiation rite for membership in a gang) and our recycling stolen from the garage. But inside the rental, very often life was lovely. Amy turned 30. I would become her husband a short time later. We took any number of photographs. Bought a massive antique stove for furniture, gathered pets. We were prose poems, curious about what we might find inside narrative.

One keeps meeting the world-as-non-sequitur through an assemblage of randomly construed facts:
    —That one of the greatest joys in my life was seeing a pair of pileated woodpeckers on Cortes Island, a place I first heard about in an Alice Munro story.
    —That I buy new shoes once every three years: Blundstones, once made in Tasmania, but now in Asia.

—Early-onset Alzheimer's: the malady my (now deceased) dentist didn't know he had, making him unable to detect advancing bone loss in my jaw. Implants were very expensive, and only a small amount was covered by insurance. I chose to proceed with the periodontal work anyway.

—That I own many, many large scrapbooks in which I keep a bestiary of bizarre news items.

—In *We Wept Without Tears*, Eliezer Eisenschmidt, a member of the Sonderkommando (the Jewish prisoners forced to remove corpses from the gas chambers at Birkenau), recalls a particularly gentle comrade "who was very sensitive and took care of the bodies of murdered children only. He'd evidently been a teacher or a writer. He looked for children's bodies only; he went into the gas chambers, and pulled out their bodies. In our jargon, a baby was called a piccolo and that became this Jew's nickname. No one knew his real name. We always called him Piccolo. He'd pick up the bodies and carry them to the pit or the furnaces."

— I was going to my night shift in the grocery store when John Lennon was shot on Monday, December 8, 1980, the news on the car radio around 10 o'clock.

It was snowing.

—Basri. The surname of an Indonesian Communist political prisoner on whose behalf I repeatedly wrote letters to Indonesian government officials on a typewriter as a member of Amnesty International when I was fifteen. Listening to Lennon's post-Beatles music made me feel I should do something about things that were happening in the world. But the Vietnam War was over, and besides, I was Canadian. I decided to join Amnesty. Now I sign online petitions with the mere click of a mouse. Has the reader seen the 2012 movie *The Act of Killing*, directed by Joshua Oppenheimer and co-directed by Christine Cynn and someone whom Wikipedia identifies as an anonymous Indonesian?

—The elderly man whose family believe (but can't prove) he molested several children, beginning with a friend of the birthday girl at a swimming party. In his late 70s, being treated for a particularly lethal form of cancer, he's going to lose his teeth because of radiation treatment. He's also lost inside dementia. When he dies, only his victims will know for certain what actually occurred. Facing his youngest daughter for the first time since his cancer diagnosis, he opened his hands wide and remarked: "Look at what I've come to!"

The intimate cynicism of the world.

I've read Proust's *In Search of Lost Time* three times; I've read *Anna Karenina* three times as well because I suspect it's Alice Munro's favourite novel. Wallace's *Infinite Jest* twice. Musil's *Man Without Qualities* once, ditto Karl Ove Knausgaard's *My Struggle*; some of Zadie Smith's essays but not a line of her fiction. Of all the Toni Morrison novels I've read, *Jazz* speaks closest to me.

She turns Hegel into a street busker.

It took me about nine weeks to read the Knausgaard from start to finish, whereas to do the same with Proust (with whom KOK has been compared) takes me the same number of *months.* I do know what this says about the two writers, but I don't know what it means about our times.

Two-thirds of the bookcases behind me were curb-snatched.

*

A mature Anna's hummingbird hovers near the sugar-water feeder; an exceptionally combative and territorial creature, it will chase off and then pursue a competitor with the dexterity of a heat-seeking missile. Its tongue resembles a thin spray of water that is also a sticky strand of a spider's web. I can hear its wings whirring, but not the vocalizations it makes, audible to Amy and Jakob, a reminder that my worsening hearing is blotting out parts of the world as I age.

*

Schadenfreude—the vice for whose sudden and immediate arrival I most revile myself.

*

Alex Trebek died not so long ago. Let's play *Jeopardy*.

Answer: This adjective characterizes my understanding of world history (See Pankaj Mishra's deconstruction of the basic historical and philosophical knowledge shared by both progressive and reactionary white intellectuals in "Grand Illusions," an essay published in the November 19, 2020, *New York Review of Books*).

Question: What is **flimsy**?

*

Jorie Graham's *Fast*. No lines more full of emptying. Except Dionne Brand's.

*

Montage: implacable: mysterious. And is it only a matter of time[8]

To be born into the ranks of the Filipino poor is to be condemned to the fatalistic knowledge of perpetual hardship and the dangerous futility of seeking improvement. Landowners dominate local governments, while deploying private armies to keep control.
  —Peter S. Goodman, "A Promise to Philippine Farmers Can Kill Them," *The New York Times,* December 29, 2019

8   until the future's splintering doppelgänger somehow appears posed in a hidden Bavarian bathtub? See the photograph taken of Lee Miller in Hitler's bath in 1945. Carolyn Burke writes: "In the most telling irony in a photograph full of ironies, Lee saw herself both in Hitler and the statuette—which recalls her modeling career and role as muse for Man, Huene, and Cocteau. Having placed this miniature Venus, armed but cut off at the knees, opposite Hitler's portrait, she turns toward her counterpart, whose raised right arm echoes her own. This sly jab at cultural clichés about the eternal feminine is complicated by Lee's knowledge that as a blue-eyed blonde, she met Hitler's aesthetic standards—which concurred with the prewar period's return to classicism. This rapidly composed scene includes her recognition that she would have been considered an Aryan, one of the hated 'Krauts.'" (Carolyn Burke, *Lee Miller: A Life*, U of Chicago P, 2005. 263.)

*

Not all spiders make webs.

*

Sentences with built-in memories.
—Don DeLillo, *Mao II*

A definition of metaphysics:
My eldest son, Jesse, then aged six: Dad, I'd like to try being someone else. I want to be other people. I could even be a piece of furniture.

*

As a child I collected trilobite fossils I found with a small hammer and chisel, tools I bought with my allowance; I wanted to be a pale-ontologist when I grew up. Years later, walking along Hadrian's Wall, I wanted to become an archaeologist. In high school, my ambition was to head to Japan after graduation and study Zen. Now I find myself a late middle-aged English professor at a small university in the middle of Canada's prairies.

My father's a snowbird who winters in Florida. He's likely one of the luckiest people to have ever lived. Born in Canada in 1939, his father was too young to have fought in the First World War, too old for the Second. Dad believes in reincarnation and maintains that when he's travelled in France, he's recognized villages in Normandy from hundreds of years ago when he used to live there.

That I suspect nothing coincides with anything, especially itself, and that I will never detect what's behind all the hidden staircases that have brought me here.

—for Don Coles, 1927 - 2017

THE SUNDAY BOOK

for Maurice Elliott

When the theme song for David Lynch's *Twin Peaks* started to play over the café's sound system, I lost my balance: it was as though something had given way in a floor upon which I'd been walking. Hastily eating breakfast, with a slight hangover, I hadn't heard the TV show's theme music since watching the final episode of the series in the early 1990s, but there it was once more. It was just after 6:00 a.m. and the music was playing on the Muzak channel belonging to the Hotel Galicja in Oświeçim, Poland, in late 2011. I was nervous about taking a series of trains that day to Prague, knowing no Polish or Czech, but this anxiety was pushed aside as I looked around at the other tables and wondered whether any of the other diners were surprised to be suddenly reminded of Laura Palmer as they ate their breakfast.

If there are few things as ordinary as travelers getting an early start on the day, eating from a buffet and maintaining quiet conversation, the confluence of *Twin Peaks* and the restaurant in which I was seated seemed incommensurate with each other. Little has demonstrated the singular violence of oblivion to me more than that moment. Everyone in the restaurant seemed insensible to the simple historical fact that what we were doing would have been utterly impossible to experience seventy years before. Meeting the eye of the blonde waitress (white blouse, modest black skirt, high heels) as I tilted my coffee cup toward her, I listened to the beginning notes of this music that originally accompanied Lynch's images of a waterfall and logging mill in the state of Washington, but was just then creating ambience for those of us dining in the traditional Stara Poczta restaurant, part of a spa which is less than 5 km from the Lager the Nazis called Auschwitz-Birkenau. I'd spent the previous two days visiting the camp, attempting sporadically to imagine what happened there, but mostly walking slowly and avoiding anyone else's eyes. If hearing the music over a plate of eggs and thin, linked sausages, some green melon—food I had chosen myself from a buffet in contrast to the near starvation imposed upon inmates during the 1940s—took me by surprise, I couldn't help but also recall another Sunday morning, this one in New Mexico in 1990, on a morning that was rich with the complexity and singular promise of a road trip. Lynn and I were heading in the direction of Ship Rock past a Navajo market, and, like many thirty-somethings in the early '90s, we were devoted fans of *Twin Peaks* and had scrambled to get a hotel room Saturday night in time to catch that week's episode. After the show, we started watching Bette Davis in *Of Human Bondage*, but went to sleep a few minutes into the movie because we were tired from a day of driving from Taos and hiking to see the Puebloan ruins at Bandelier Park near Los Alamos.

After the song ended in the Polish restaurant and I got ready to leave, I thought of how absurd it was to recall the pleasant associations I attached to Lynch's occult murder mystery while I was having breakfast in that formal, pristine restaurant so near the former concentration camp. Only forty-five years had passed between the initial airing of *Twin Peaks* in 1990 and the time the Russians entered what was left of the camp, freeing Primo Levi and the few hundred others who remained after the Nazis had fled. The restaurant had some antique furniture that must have predated the war. The blunt mystery of time seems corrosive and banal: one day the present was January 27, 1945—the day the Russians liberated the inmates—and on another day a small group of people were having breakfast on November 6, 2011.

*

Sundays began to be important to me when I worked nights stocking shelves in a grocery store; the start of my five-day work week was Sunday evening at 10:00, and the shift ended at 8:00 the next morning. Each Sunday felt ruined because a day off quickly turned into a night shift. And, being young, I was often up late on Saturday nights, making it impossible to get enough rest during the next day. I was just out of high school, living with my girlfriend Cindy, who worked rotating shifts as a nurse's aide at an old-age home. We were new to working full time, and if we were surprised by how much energy it consumed, we were also amazed at our independence. Our exhausting, repetitive, and sometimes demeaning work met expenses and allowed us to save money so we could eventually travel to Europe and then start university. This was in the early 80s, when young people still read Charles Bukowski,

50

sometimes Margaret Laurence, Somerset Maugham, and books like Tom Robbins's *Still Life with Woodpecker*, writers and books that are now mostly ignored. We listened to mid-career Leonard Cohen on LPs and somehow managed without credit cards. Cut art calendars apart to decorate our apartment. Watched my parents get divorced. Smoked cigarettes and occasionally skated through most of a weekend on some tabs of LSD.

I was going to be a writer and she was going to be a painter.

During those nights at the grocery store, I'd call her from the store's phone at the Customer Service desk before she went to sleep, and I promised myself that one day I'd be sitting at a typewriter when it was 4:00 in the morning, sipping wine rather than working my ass off to fulfill the quota the grocery store's management insisted upon. The quota used a formula that determined how many cardboard boxes had to be sliced open on each shift so that cans, bottles, and bags could be priced individually and then rammed on the shelves. No scanning devices for bar codes then. No cell phones. I can remember eating peanut butter sandwiches and reading *Zen and the Art of Motorcycle Maintenance* on my lunch break at 3:00 a.m. in the staff room in the store's basement while the other two members of the night crew played gin rummy. As for Cindy, her difficulty was that many of the people in her care were mentally ill. Eventually an ancient woman she'd slowly befriended attacked her—biting and scratching her arms—and she quit the nursing home to take up a job as a waitress, where she had to wear black pumps and a brown uniform for a country-style inn.

*

Only a few Novembers ago, Cindy sent me this email, referring to Cohen's death, subject heading "he's gone":

Haven't heard from you for a while. I hope you are ok. I had to write to you on news of Leonard Cohen.
Immobilised by Trump's election and then the loss of him. Sad week.
And I remember us in Hydra… looking for his house… so young, so long ago, but I still have the images of streets, of the port, the room, the food, the blue water, and sunburns and the topless tanned woman on the rock (we were shades of pink, she was golden). Even a few jellyfish, but they didn't sting.
Take care, dear friend.
C

She'd written this from her home in Spain, just a week after her fifty-fifth birthday. She didn't become a painter; instead, she's got a doctorate in sustainable agriculture, is married to a chemistry professor, and has two teenage boys. Speaks Spanish. But my memory is different from hers on the jellyfish: I can remember snorkeling, coming up to the surface, and seeing that I was surrounded by many pink jellyfish, their tendrils like negligees, and they did sting. But the water was so cold you didn't feel it immediately.

*

Today it's early on a Sunday morning in Regina, Saskatchewan (where I've lived for over twenty years), and I'm drinking coffee, writing on a laptop instead of a typewriter. I've been listening to the *Twin Peaks* soundtrack on iTunes because I've been trying to remember more clearly those two very different Sunday mornings, one taking place in New Mexico and the other, more than twenty years later, in Poland.

When I arrived at the hotel in Oświeçim late Friday afternoon, I asked a cab driver waiting there if he could take me to Auschwitz. He spoke no English, and so the concierge inquired of me which Auschwitz I wanted to visit: I or II. Until then, I hadn't any sense of the camp's geography, and a man who'd just come in to the hotel, clearly also a tourist, informed me that Auschwitz I was the one with the *Arbeit Macht Frei* sign and the other was Birkenau. Given that both places would be closed soon, I asked him which one I should go to first. Auschwitz I, the older part of the camp, he advised. What made me make the trip to Auschwitz-Birkenau nearly a decade ago now is the subject of another essay in this book ("Contours: In Search of Etty Hillesum"). I will say, though, that for most of my adult life, I've read about the Holocaust, and one of the reasons I went was that it seemed necessary to go to Poland as I pondered what our obligation is to those lives that were struck down in such misery. If going there and walking the grounds can turn the abstraction of the camp's name into a place with gravel roads and enlarged photographs of what took place during the summer of 1944 so the visitor can pause, look around, and contrast a precise image from the past with his or her present, one soon understands that the memorial site itself is a kind of non-place. What's there is the soil beneath one's feet or the endless ruins of barracks with their broken-down chimneys. Nearly all of Auschwitz's victims are nameless now, and we don't have antennae capable of discerning either them or the ruthless emptiness contained in the word "gone."

And how, after all, can one accept not to know? We read books on Auschwitz. The wish of all in the camps, the last wish: know what has happened, do not forget, and at the same time never will you know.

—Maurice Blanchot, *The Writing of the Disaster*

Yes, we read. Books that we read for the first time, and also those to which we keep returning—the work of Etty Hillesum, Jean Améry, Primo Levi—and all of these books are important to pass on to young people, those who weren't formed by the twentieth century. Every other year, I teach a course on Holocaust literature. I always include Charlotte Delbo's *Auschwitz and After* because its blend of poetry, memoir, and fiction provides her with a number of lenses to give shape to her experience, both as an inmate and when she returned to France. In one poem, she's unequivocally clear about the sensibility we must take within ourselves, those of us who lead safe lives long after the war ended. A survivor of Birkenau, she dares us to imagine being judged by those who perished. Their deaths will be made meaningless, Delbo asserts, looking directly at her reader, if "you live / doing nothing with your life." These lines are a prayer reaching out as much as they're already a curse. Knowing that no one can reply adequately to this admonition, Delbo offers it as a way for her readers to ponder the immensities of what sometimes happens to other people. While nothing can be done for those who were murdered, Delbo challenges her readers to keep in mind the extraordinary luxury of having some choice in how we now live our lives.

*

When I think of what Delbo says, however—that we should consider our lives as they might be judged by those who died at Auschwitz—I feel panic and self-loathing. Self-loathing because I once read her poem one afternoon after binge-watching *The Walking Dead* from 9:00 p.m. the previous night until robins stirred me from the couch just before dawn. Maybe there's no harm in doing something like this occasionally, but as I sat outside, listening to the birdsong and taking in the tree branches that were only beginning to show through the dark, I knew that the past eight or nine hours in front of the television had been symptomatic of something larger.

For the previous decade, I'd gone to many places to write: a miniature portable office that sat in the driveway, a hotel room in Saskatoon, any place I could feel unsupervised. Aided by a room's emptiness, wine, and the joy of drinking alone—though it wasn't simply to have fun getting pissed. I needed to burrow into a place that could only be found by hooking onto and catching a piece of music and then playing it obsessively while working on something. Because of the filmmaker Fassbinder and an old friend of mine, now dead, I once listened to one of Kraftwerk's songs several dozen times while writing a poem. When I finished the poem, having had "Radioactivity" on repeat for the whole night, it was dawn. Light was happening several kilometers above me, and it stretched from what presses from Maiden Castle, an Iron-Age hill fort in southern England, into the world we inhabit. I know that people just getting up sometimes see dawn as a good thing… but if you've not been asleep and actually see dawn, it shows a world you wish to join, but it also evicts you in the same moment. This complicated light seems to be where painters and photographers live. But you can't do this for long: write all night while sipping wine. Eventually, lassitude arrives. For some years, I was productive working like this, but then I got into the pattern of writing a long love-email to my wife upon arriving, and then staying awake most of the night, working on some lines for a few hours and then watching R.E.M. videos on YouTube before uncomfortably sleeping on the small couch in my sublet downtown. I'd wander home in that crystalline fog drinking confers. That particular morning after losing the night to *The Walking Dead*, sipping what was left of the previous night's tequila, I looked once again at the fact that I wasn't living the way I'd hoped when I stocked shelves on the night shift in the grocery store more than thirty years before.

Alongside this revulsion I also felt panic. It's been 14 years since I've published a book, and it's out of print. My short-term memory seems to be evaporating, and my working vocabulary feels arthritic.[9] This continual decay can partially be attributed to aging, likely added to by substance abuse as well as decades of anxiety and depression. I'm not ready to face getting older, and my being unprepared disappoints and angers me. I once desired to gain autonomy from myself, from everything, but I've remained an adolescent instead. I've lived lazily. The story's an old one, though it's surprising all the same to discover how mystifying, even stupefying, it is to abruptly feel this sense of solitary idiocy at becoming the late middle-aged man I didn't have the capacity to imagine during

---

9   I keep a list of words I observe others using that I realise I haven't used for years: "forsake"—Zadie Smith, "Man vs. Corpse"; "salient"—Tony Judt, *Memory Chalet*; "ensuing"—Karl Ove Knausgaard, *My Struggle*; and so on.

my twenties. When I was younger, I reacted to the future as others likely do: with desire, apprehension, and nonchalance. I tried to protect myself by holding onto the nebulous ambition of wanting "to write," whatever that meant. I've disavowed consequences almost entirely and have lived carelessly through three decades, never noticing how harmless it seems… to keep coasting, to keep postponing the moment when you recognize that, through ceaseless distraction and evasion, you've not only wasted enormous chunks of your life, you're also on the cusp of abandoning it. And there's no one else to blame.

*

To replay the *Twin Peaks* soundtrack is to glance safely into a deep nihilism: imagine Delbo as an inmate standing at roll call in the winter, and then give her the capacity to observe the diners in the spa's restaurant, each of us accustomed to Muzak, some of us familiar with American popular culture. It might seem to her that, as far as the future is concerned, Birkenau never took place: time has scrubbed clean everything that happened there. The fundamental inequities of history and geography, their arbitrary nature, are utterly stark. Yet I don't think Delbo would deny any of us our subjective lives. How are we to measure the value of personal experience within the context of what she says? How can it be used as a tool to examine the sliver of reality that we inhabit?

As I listen to the soundtrack, replay parts of the show in my mind, I realize that several significant events in my life have coincidentally happened on Sundays, and if I'm to make any kind of effort to break free of self-delusion, I need to work harder at reclaiming my memory. I want to scrutinize what kind of cage I've chosen to walk into. Perhaps if I return to that gathering of Sundays that can be differentiated from the blank weeks and months that, invisibly surrounding them, are mostly lost to me—perhaps then, I can recast these small bits of memory so that an otherwise seemingly squandered life can become more than elapsed time rife with inconsequence. Not that this task is meant to ameliorate anything or to wander solely into autobiography. Like everyone, I've encountered some things that are much larger than me, and I want to liberate them from my private associations to then try to examine what they are.

YOU DON'T HAVE TO DO THIS

Sunday, October 7, 1990

Because she loved driving, Lynn drove the pristine burgundy Ford we rented in Albuquerque, a vehicle that took us from D.H. Lawrence's grave site—a chapel resplendent with a kitsch eagle, Lawrence's ashes interred in a hanging urn, and his wife Frieda conveniently buried outside—east of Taos to Bandolier and then on to Farmington, where we scrambled from hotel to hotel (no cell phones then) to find the last available room in the city (owing to a Shriner's convention), finally tucking into *Twin Peaks*. Rising early that Sunday morning to go to Arizona's Canyon de Chelly, we passed a busy, dusty market on the outskirts of town where the desert scrub began, and later we could see Ship Rock in an empty-but-somehow-compressed landscape we'd only imagined before.

The sky was overcast, near rain. Not lethargic but heavy nonetheless, yet wonderfully resonant with apparent weightlessness. We were utterly elated to be alone together, travelling as comfortable and unobserved strangers through those enormous spaces for the first and only time, not knowing that we wouldn't encounter such blind, towering emptiness again until we moved from southern Ontario to Saskatchewan with our infant baby, Andy, seven years later. Along the way we took too few photos of the sublimely tilted, reticent landscape, the car occasionally shaken with hammering, grit-filled wind, and listened to David Bowie on CDs we'd brought with us from Toronto. We sang along with him about never having done good things, or bad things, and did the two of us (or only me) wonder what these things, especially the transgressive ones, might one day come to mean for us?

Arriving early Sunday afternoon at Canyon de Chelly, we noticed a small chain across the gravel trail leading from the parking lot with a sign on it saying that, because George Bush had vetoed a budget, the National Park was closed. It took some convincing, but I managed to persuade Lynn that we were very far from Washington D.C. and that we should simply step over the chain and descend to the canyon. The entire hike took about three hours, and apart from a few Navajo men at the bottom of the canyon, some horses, and a barely visible black dog in the distance, no one else was there. I wish I could summon what it felt like to look up the cliff from the canyon's sandy floor and photograph the Anasazi White House Ruins that could almost have been their famous black-and-white photo taken in the nineteenth century. There could hardly be a world more different from the one that had us lying in bed watching the newest episode of *Twin Peaks* the night before. I felt like an intruder. From the floor of the canyon, we could see a grey sea-fall of light barely moving between the clouds and the flat, mostly dry riverbed, filled with horse hoof-prints, upon which we stood.

Long before the legality of our divorce was signified by a document passed between lawyers, Lynn must have understood that our marriage had ceased entirely the moment she stood in the hallway of our house in Saskatchewan and said, "you don't have to do this," only to encounter my rejection of her as I turned and walked out the front door to go to a one-room apartment in another part of the city. There's a terrible moment in the movie *No Country for Old Men* when a woman who's just buried her mother returns to her home to find a man sitting quietly in her bedroom, a man who is there to kill her. "You don't have to do this," she tells him, and he replies, "People always say that… they say, 'You don't have to do this.'" When I saw that scene in a Cineplex, I automatically heard the same words as they were said to me in the autumn of 2003. *Don't do this* is so different from *you don't have to do this*; the latter opens up the possibility of change, of freedom, through the necessity of engaging with the other person while they are alongside you during that present moment. Except that the person committing the act against the other person refuses to participate in this shared moment of time, or even acknowledge it, because they have already made up their mind. There's something monstrous in this egotism. I wonder if there isn't something deliberately pitiless, something malicious, in me that was manifested in my capacity to resolutely ignore Lynn's request to rethink my choice.

In her helplessness and grief that autumn, she asked me—amidst all the anger I directed against her—to tell her something good about herself, to show her that I still had some happy memories from our marriage. I've sometimes wondered what event or period of time she imagined I would evoke. I confirmed that we'd been happy often, but specifically referred to that trip we'd once taken to New Mexico. She wrote back to me—this exchange was over email—saying that, yes, the trip had been special and that she could still remember waiting for me at the bottom of the ladder that led to the kiva at Bandolier, and that she had felt elated to be precisely there in New Mexico waiting on the trail for her husband, with, as she put it, all of our lives yet ahead of us. I didn't know then how capable I was of the commonplace, even casual, brutality that allowed me to leave her and our two children.

The ladder to which Lynn referred was made from local pine. The bark had been planed off the tree trunks so the ladder they'd been shaped into, bolted to the rough, porous cliff, had become bleached and smooth. Almost entirely vertical, cool to the touch, this ladder led to some petroglyphs and a Puebloan kiva that people with a phobia of heights, such as Lynn, miss unfortunately. I would never have gone up, quickly placing hand over hand on the twenty or more rungs as I knew I must, had I not had to take work as a roofer some years before, a job which forced me to learn that one has to steadily ignore one's imagination to overcome fear. My point here isn't to applaud my courage in getting over a phobia; I suspect anyone, given financial necessity, can do the same. What concerns me more is how deeply contingency shapes our lives. I'd gotten the roofing job because someone I'd known in the small town where I grew up was working with the company in Toronto. Without his recommendation, it would never have occurred to me to apply. More importantly, Lynn and I wouldn't have been in Bandolier Park in New Mexico, she waiting for me down below on the trail, if not for a passage in John Fowles's *Daniel Martin*, in which the novel's eponymous narrator speaks so beguilingly of this landscape. When we'd wondered where to travel for our first week-long vacation since marrying five years earlier, I read her a few sentences from the Fowles, and she agreed we should go. When, thirteen years later, Lynn turned her waiting for me on the trail into an almost allegorical account of our marriage, one that showcased her fidelity and patience, she gave the trip a sense of inevitability that it didn't have at the time.

Returning to Albuquerque on Monday from the ancient solitude of the canyon, we noticed something odd in the horizon but couldn't identify what it was. The far-off sky was filled with dots that we could make out through the dust and insects smeared on the car's windshield. Having travelled to New Mexico on impulse, we didn't know that the weekend we went to Taos corresponded with the beginning of Albuquerque's hot air balloon festival. We drove to the fairgrounds and then walked amidst the balloons that cold, bright autumn day, some of the balloons about to take off, others lying on their sides, waiting to be inflated. Overhead, the gleaming blue sky was crammed deep with them. Dozens and dozens of balloons; I don't know how they maneuvered around each other—there were so many. I can't imagine what it would have been like to be standing up there in the basket with the pilot. Some were surprisingly fantastic in their designs: her favourite was a hummingbird; mine showed a white profile of Anubis leading Horus against a pitch-black background. On the flight home to Ontario we read of an accident that had happened on the Saturday we'd been hiking—two men (aged forty-six and thirty-two) had been killed as a result of their balloon drifting into some power lines—and fifteen years in the future, I would write a poem to our nine-year-old child Andy in which the most important image is an auditory one: the singular roaring sound the flames in a hot air balloon make as the fire keeps it afloat.

Twenty-three years from the trip to New Mexico, in 2013, I would take Andy to see the Gay Pride Parade on a Sunday in Chicago, where they enthused about the Dykes on Bikes, topless women with black tape crisscrossed over their nipples, leaning back as they rode their hogs, resplendent in their defiance and sense of fun. When the parade ended in the late afternoon, leaving the streets disheveled and almost pale with over-satiated light, Sheriff of Cook County prison buses with grills on their windows dropped off numerous prison convicts to sweep up the trash that freedom, excess, and garish irony had left behind.

I keep returning to Lynn's elation in 1990 that we had all of our lives yet ahead of us. To trust the future, to imbue a present-day pleasure with the addition of a safe future, is so fundamental to our capacity to survive. It's such a necessary drug. I've rarely felt secure when I've looked ahead, though I well understand the powerful rush of joy derived from anticipating a shared future with someone, how sustaining it can be. But the present itself is unwieldy; there's so much more to it than what we take it for. And the mind gets stunned each time it has to relearn how remote from the present the ceaselessly unimaginable future always becomes. How untrustworthy time is… and how brutal when events eject someone from what they thought was the trajectory of their life.

Let's pause here.

What to do with the present while writing a long piece of prose such as this one? Yesterday (March 15, 2020) I sent an email to Cindy because it seems that Spain is getting hit hard by COVID-19, but she hasn't replied. And also yesterday, instead of stocking shelves in a grocery store as I once did, I joined many other shoppers trying to hoard supplies. It must be chaos for the night shift. Saskatchewan is slowly shutting down. What will the world experience if most countries follow France's lockdown with people confined to their homes? Of European countries, Italy is suffering the most.

As airlines cease flying travelers, there's a gathering plume of silence in the sky, and I think of visiting Pompeii as a child… and here is the savagery of human time: if one could stand in Pompeii's amphitheater today, emptied of tourists and their selfies, and move an instant backwards to a steady stream of yesterdays slowly rushing by, eventually my family would appear—the showers were cold in the dusty, dusty campground, I recall—and then less than a year before our visit, Pink Floyd recorded a concert with no audience on the floor of the amphitheater in 1971. According to Wikipedia, the place could seat the entire population of the city. Slip back 1,892 years as the twin of Eurydice, slip past the slow immediacy of tightening ash, and then here's some light coming from the heart of the sun: imagine four people: a Roman citizen and his wife at the games; two gladiators facing off. The couple actually existed and today stares at us from a fresco; once safely inside their lives, they watch people die in combat, everyone's few years of sheltered (or violent) life beginning to scatter before the eruption—

BRUEGEL'S *HUNTERS IN THE SNOW* ↔ *KONZENTRATIONSLAGER MAUTHAUSEN*

July 20, 2014

A postcard of Bruegel's *Hunters in the Snow* is taped to the yellow wall to my right, everything bright with autumn sun. It's not the only postcard here—another shows Jean Améry posed with an almost-finished cigarette, his face looking as though Rembrandt had done the portrait— and I wonder how many people have decorated a room with Bruegel's familiar image. And under what circumstances? There must be any number of us who have chosen to do this identical thing: keep these hunters, their exhausted dogs, the ice skaters far below, keep all of them in a place to which we often return.

If one looks into the slightly staged photograph of where Dylan Thomas liked to work—scrunched paper dutifully collecting on the floor—one notices *Hunters in the Snow* in his writing studio. I didn't know of his interest in Bruegel when I saw the painting in Vienna's Kunsthistoriches Museum; if I had, I would have spent a few moments looking at it with Thomas in mind. Thomas must have known W. H. Auden's poem that replies to Bruegel. Did it influence how he thought about this painting?[10] Or was he able to put Auden aside and observe this winter scene as though it was appearing outside his own window?

It's an odd thing that when people look at a painting, their eyes take in a shared image, and yet the particular effect it has on each person must become instantly personal, idiosyncratic, and remain invisible to others. I realize that most don't find this situation to be of much concern, but our sense of reality is greatly reduced because we habitually ignore the singularity of individual experience. We oversimplify. Perhaps living within the communal sphere of screen culture results in imaginative sloth: it's easy to deem one's own thoughts normative. Bruegel's huge painting (1.17 x 1.62 meters) has existed for centuries, remaining separate from generations of viewers who aren't allowed to get too close to it there on the wall: it would be fascinating, and quite likely dislocating, to know their reactions, both when they saw it (or a reproduced image) for the first time, and then later, when it might occur to them to think about the winter scene again.

In *Facing the Extreme*, a study on the concentration camps, Tzvetan Todorov mentions how two Ravensbrück inmates, Milena Jesenská (only two decades earlier a recipient of Kafka's love letters) and Margarete Buber-Neumann, tore a reproduction of the painting from a magazine and stuck it to a wall in their barrack "as 'a protest against [their] condition as prisoners.'" It's likely that at least Jesenská had seen the original, but what was her reaction when she unexpectedly saw the picture in a magazine abandoned by an SS officer? How long were these women permitted to keep it? If someone today stands in that large room full of Bruegels, what kind of correspondence can there be between that experience and Jesenská's, going from painting to painting when she lived in Vienna during the 1920s? I'll return to the question of how Bruegel might have regarded the camps later; for now, let me note John Berger's belief that Bruegel wouldn't have been surprised to learn of the new forms of violence that appeared during the twentieth century. Human indifference to the suffering of others was something he seemed to have thought about often.

*

Some years before going to Vienna, I began the habit of observing people in art museums. This started when I noticed a couple

---

10   There's also a photograph of Auden above Thomas's desk at Laugharne, though from our twenty-first-century perspective, it's of a *young* Auden; at the time Thomas hung it up, it would have been a contemporary image.

standing still while numerous others milled around them one day in the Museum of Modern Art (MoMA) in New York City. They were looking into a Chagall painting, and from behind it was apparent that they were elderly, their stature and clothing signifying acceptable health and an ordinary amount of available money. Because they paused as they took in the floating lovers—rather than hurrying through the gallery snapping pictures on phones as many others did—I imagined that they'd lived in the city all their lives, had grandchildren, and were looking at this specific painting because they'd done so at various points in their lives. Even though their history and personal attachment to Chagall was something I was fabricating, I envied them almost as much as I'd ever envied anyone. How fortunate they were to be able to return to this painting (or the nearby Giacometti sculptures) as often as daily life would permit; and how fortunate, too, that they had been able to live alongside these modernist works when they were relatively new. They themselves had aged with the artworks. As someone who was a child when Giacometti died, I'll never understand what modernism meant in its time, and as a visitor from the Canadian prairies, I'll never be able to study the paintings at the MoMA carefully because I must rely on my memory and reproductions, rather than being able to go back repeatedly to that unique space—perhaps a meter in length—that exists between a painting and its viewer.[11] There are far worse things to regret, of course, but as far as paintings are concerned, I'm only ever a tourist.

While in Vienna in 2014 to attend a conference (giving a paper on Nathan Englander's short story "What We Talk About When We Talk About Anne Frank"), I skipped most of the panels. Instead, I took in paintings, strolled with a friend from Regina who by coincidence was also doing research in the city, visited the Hotel Imperial because Rainer

---

11   The *Wikipedia* entry on Alberto Giacometti quotes him saying: "I've been fifty thousand times to the Louvre. I have copied everything in drawing, trying to understand." People interested in books or movies don't have this problem; it is unimaginable to have to travel across the Atlantic to read John Ashbery's "Self-Portrait in a Convex Mirror," though one can gain an appreciation for the poem's nuances by observing Parmigianino's painting. Birding, like looking at paintings, requires proximity; it's obviously dependent on numerous variables: timing, skill, geography. Sadly, birdwatching is also very precarious: to see a pair of wood ducks in Regina's Wascana Lake at dusk is to mourn in advance the potential destruction of the habitat belonging to these elegant creatures.

Maria Rilke had frequented it,[12] and searched out sites where the Nazis had wielded their power, including Freud's residence where, unknown to me until I went, the Nazis had stored Jews (after Freud and his family had emigrated) before deporting them. Aware that I might never find myself in Vienna again, I went to see *Hunters in the Snow* twice. That sentence is innocuous, straightforward, and factual, yet it feels awkward, immediately embodying a kind of peculiar, unwelcome irony that is omnipresent whenever one travels to places where atrocities have occurred. Because almost all of the Jewish deportees would never return to their Wien, my own sheltered situation was obvious. If no one can be held responsible for the way time obliterates everything that happens, proximity to places where terrible suffering has occurred seems nevertheless to make one feel accountable, and something that's akin to self-reproach becomes as inevitable as it's likely necessary. Against the uneasiness one feels while walking through squares that held crowds cheering Hitler in 1938, one intuits that Bruegel's paintings offer something else—call it a blurring of the personal and the sublime. If the images can't ameliorate loss, the vast spaces they usually depict open up a kind of freedom that is antithetical to the violent impulses exploited by Nazism.

While staring into its sky, I felt a nudge on my right shoulder: a younger colleague to whom I'd been introduced the day before at the conference. This colleague, the writer Steve Gronert Ellerhof, left soon after we met accidentally in front of the painting, as he'd booked a train to Zurich that afternoon because he wanted to pass a few days visiting places where Carl Jung had lived. It was from Zurich that the *Jäger im Schnee* postcard to my right was sent. Steve wrote it sitting in front of Joyce's grave. We recognized each other as two people impelled to merge the inner world of reading writers no longer living with contemporary geographic reality by going on private pilgrimages, though we haven't seen each other since then.[13] We were also particularly drawn

---

12   The hotel was almost empty, its opulence awaiting someone other than me. Alone in the mirror-filled café on the street level, I toasted Rilke with a cognac and imagined him writing—as Malte Laurids Brigge—"Is it possible that we thought we had to retrieve what happened before we were born?" Kafka stayed in this hotel with Jesenská for four days in 1920. What happens as one day metamorphoses into the next? Hitler worked in the hotel as a casual labourer when he was broke, but then returned in triumph during the *Anschluss* in 1938. Knowing this history, Simon Wiesenthal chose to celebrate his 90th birthday party there in 1998.

13   Steve knew that I was going to Amsterdam the next day to visit places where Etty Hillesum lived, and he subsequently pointed me to Sonu Shamdasani's remarks

to this specific Bruegel painting, though the huge room was crowded with his work. Whether aesthetic experience can actually be shared and then communicated is perhaps unknowable, though much seems to be at stake in whatever effect *Hunters in the Snow* has on its viewers. Lars von Trier begins *Melancholia* (his film conjoining depression with interplanetary destruction), by showing the corpses of birds slowly falling down a screen that then mutates alarmingly into *Hunters in the Snow*, which then darkens, quickly burning into black ash. The film's opening sequence (itself a tribute to Tarkovsky's *Solaris*) implies that, if one had the capacity to rescue two phenomena from earth's imminent destruction, a case could be made that birds and this painting especially merit preservation, a position that makes considerable sense to me.

*

Two days separated my visits to the museum, and in between them I went to Mauthausen, the fortress-like concentration camp near Linz, built of concrete and granite by inmates and designated by Himmler to be one of the Reich's harshest camps owing to the forced labour in its quarry. Vast quantities of stone needed to be lifted by prisoners if Hitler was to realize his architectural fantasies. But before I went to Mauthausen, I'd gone to the Judenplatz Holocaust Memorial. Designed by Rachel Whiteread, this gleaming white monument is a large rectangular sculpture that's made mostly of stone books with their spines facing inwards, so their titles can't be read. Around the base are names identifying the 41 places where Austria's Jews were transported, from Auschwitz to Zamość.

During that summer (coincidentally the centenary of World War I), the nearby Jewish museum devoted an exhibition to Amy Winehouse, and her life-sized portrait faced the monument. Among other memorabilia, the exhibition included her favourite guitar and one of the dresses in which she'd performed. Beneath the square, and precisely below the monument, are the ruins of a partially excavated medieval synagogue that was destroyed in a fifteenth-century pogrom. Standing on the paving stones, trying to imagine the different lives people have brought to the square, one is reminded that much of reality is undetectable to our

---

that Jung came "to the view that one has to conceive of one's life both in response to the dead, and in terms of one's own becoming dead, so there's a sense of suspension as between two mysteries, which relativizes one's own existence."

senses, and yet there it is, a densely crowded tumble of incorporeal activity pressing in. Past and present blurred together in the July heat, the relentlessly blue sky, including but also entirely independent of any individual viewpoint. As conceptual art, alight with sunshine that afternoon, the monument becomes a kind of time-telescope, pointing toward what we can't see with our eyes—except that this telescope doesn't reveal stars or planets, but rather is directed at the empty spaces between them.

As I read the names of the various camps, so did a nearby couple, but apart from us and the Lessing statue, the square was unoccupied. I couldn't catch their eyes as they peered at the monument. What imperatives or impulses were they obeying as they scanned the words inset in the stone? Intimating people and events that clamor for a passerby's recognition, these place names summon our ignorance of what happened to each of these 65,000 individuals.[14] And the words themselves must shift with each visitor. When I read "Auschwitz," I recalled some details from books and documentaries, including the work of Charlotte Delbo, alongside the impressions left from a trip I'd taken to the camp a few years before. If what transpired near the small town of Oświęcim during the 1940s seemed very far away just then from Vienna and Amy Winehouse, living in the early twenty-first century means that various companies offer a day trip between the two locations.

The word *Zamość* on the monument was meaningless to me; my mind summoned only the shape of the word, its lettering intimating a vaguely eastern-European blur. My incapacity to render the word into anything precise prompted a peculiar blend of guilt and curiosity. My reading of the word was superfluous beside the way that perpetrators and victims would have been able to embody the place name into associations specific to them. Whiteread's monument thereby severs us from what we normally take as the simple act of reading, an act that requires us to assimilate the information presented in a text. As we read the

---

14   To think more deeply about the way this monument communicates the impossibility of commemorating these people as individuals, one might turn to Jean-François Lyotard's *The Differend*, which argues that the word *Auschwitz* cannot be used as a "speculative name," and furthermore, the various names on the sculpture actually eradicate the notion of a communal "we." According to Lyotard, "in the concentration camps, there would have been no subject in the first person plural." I largely accept Lyotard's analysis; that said, ordinary experience maintains the necessary fiction that an onlooker—as a member of the communal "we" —can grasp the gist of the monument's purpose, which is to point to the fact that actual people perished at specific geographic locations.

place names, we need to envision those deported—some of whom must have stood in the square at some point in their lives, but not with the nearby image of a recently-living Amy Winehouse looking on. (The only Austrian Jew I could imagine with any clarity while standing there was Jean Améry, who must have crossed the square in which I was paused, though he committed suicide before the monument was made.)

I went twice to the Judenplatz; the first time I read the word *Mauthausen* carved into the base, the word was restricted to those scant details I remembered from *The 186 Steps: Mauthausen*, a collection of testimonials that I'd perused back in Saskatchewan. But when I returned to the memorial two days later, I'd actually visited the camp, and so the word shifted, gathered a different density, becoming fundamentally altered from the first time I'd read it.[15] I'd gone up and down the safely redesigned (and unsoiled) staircase, alone in the morning sun, carrying nothing heavier than my nearly empty backpack, full water bottle, and camera. Looked at photographs in the museum and tried to imagine the moments when they were taken. Upon leaving—an action denied to inmates—I bought a history of the camp and a postcard showing Ewa Kaja's sculpture titled *Gone*. Numerous finely detailed bald heads, eyes shut, almost buried by snow—as if they've been guillotined—a long line of them that blurs off into the distance. Just as these sculptures occupy physical space, they exert a fraying anxiety caused by the historical particulars of their origins, origins to which we have no access.

*

It's an uncanny coincidence that both Bruegel's painting and Mauthausen's quarry conspicuously place the viewer in a situation where one gazes into an immense space. Looking at the huge scene depicted in *Hunters in the Snow*, the retina takes an undiluted image straight to the brain, but the brain doesn't have to subdue what the eye sees, filter

---

15   It wasn't only the word *Mauthausen* that seemed different. The massive, stark memorials at the camp, most of them national monuments commemorating their respective citizens, manifest an entirely different sensibility than Whiteread's sculpture does. This sensibility is hard to isolate, but one realizes that these monuments are derived from a particular commemorative aesthetic that's long vanished. Anger, defiance, and grief announce something of the heroic, usually involving the human form, and referring to the nationality of victims, whereas Whiteread's unreadable library disappears into itself, leaves the public square, and moves past mourning into a deepening oblivion. No one can be inside the sculpture to read the books' titles.

it, and then somehow re-imagine, somehow overlay what's directly in front of you with what's missing as it does at Mauthausen. In trying to envision something of the camp's seven-year history, one's imagination is utterly paltry. In Bruegel, however, the open space into which the central magpie is about to plummet moves the eye into the winter scene, which in turn invites the viewer to consider the miraculous nature of motion itself—and how, for us sentient beings, time and motion coalesce. The hunters are paused mid-step, and their few footprints remain for us to see as they head down the hill, but what motion actually entails—not the heaviness of walking through snow exactly, but how one moment changes into another—is beyond my comprehension. If time seems fundamentally unintelligible, however, we can at least gape at colour. And this sky holds a cryptic green out to us that exists *only* in this location, its majesty deserving a new word. The sky's "rizzened" green, then, is reflected in the cuts scored by skaters in the pond's ice, and this tug and pull between the all-encompassing, ruminating air and the pedestrian frozen water somehow makes the viewer quicken to sensual reality: how tree bark, toes wedged in skates, or a dog's cold fur can feel remarkable. These men and their dogs have a weariness that we all know, the sort that spreads from the spine; their frustration at day's end is palpable. The hunt has been mostly unsuccessful. Because none of the people in the painting turn our way, thereby confronting us as viewers, we might maintain the illusion that we could almost step into the winter dusk. Even if the world depicted is recognizable, however, it is enclosed within a different conception of geographical space than ours, and this itself keeps us intricately separate from it.

Because I'd recently flown from Regina to Calgary to Amsterdam to Vienna, I'd been reminded of jet fuel's distinctive, greasy odor, and I realised that this smell was missing from Bruegel's world. And if winter is less punishing for Canadians today than it was for these hunters because of our technology, global warming has fundamentally altered the seasons that Bruegel knew.[16] (One reason why I might never see the painting again is that I must learn to cut down on air travel, given how flights increase emissions.) A further change, one that would have concerned Bruegel greatly, is the experience of geographic simultaneity as transmitted through the contemporary media. In 1565 no one in this Flemish town could have known of the siege of Kuragano taking place during

---

16   Adam Gopnik observes that Bruegel's painting was an "occasional" one, responding to the little ice age that occurred between the 16th and 18th centuries.

Japan's Sengoku period, but a TV in my hotel room told me instantly of Malaysia Airline Flight 117, a plane that had been shot down over Ukraine shortly after it left Amsterdam's Schiphol airport, a luxurious place where I'd eaten a sushi breakfast during a layover a few days earlier. I'd return twice more to this airport before departing Europe for home, noticing memorial flowers in one of its hallways.[17]

Both Berger and Auden are attuned to Bruegel's attention to the ethical quandaries simultaneity foists on us. Auden points to Bruegel's portrayal of the "human position" suffering takes in "Musée des Beaux Arts," though he takes Bruegel to mean that a representation of reality must acknowledge suffering and apathy equally, whereas Berger refutes this notion of harmony. Because Berger's argument extends to the fundamental concerns of this essay, let me cite it at some length. Calling Bruegel "the most unforgiving artist who ever lived," Berger sees his paintings as collecting

> the evidence for a prosecution which he had no sure reason for believing would ever be mounted…. [Bruegel] had a conscience born historically too soon for the knowledge that might justify it…. Bruegel … understood that not to resist is to be indifferent, that to forget or not to know is also to be indifferent and that to be indifferent is to condone. This … is why Bruegel's paintings are more relevant to… the concentration camps than almost any painted since.

Berger's insight that an individual conscience can exist independently from a culture's ideology and the historical experience available to it implies not only that the "indifference" Bruegel portrayed needs to be approached through the lens of twentieth-century atrocities, but also that conscience paradoxically has both universal and locally historical dimensions. (Had Auden known of the camps when he wrote his poem, would he have written it differently? I believe that he would have.) Given technological advances in communication, we are audiences to disasters and violent events occurring in real time alongside us, but when they take place in faraway geographic locations they implicitly raise the ethical responsibilities of spectatorship, a challenge that seems to be a recent

---

17   These commemorative flowers should perhaps be thought of in conjunction with Jérôme Sessini's photographs of the flight's victims, some still fastened into their seats lying on a field.

historical phenomenon.[18] Thinking about Nazism in conjunction with Bruegel suggests that we need to expand this notion of simultaneity to include the past. But what are the obligations of the living to familiarize ourselves with past suffering? How can we avoid a present-day indifference that has the corollary of condoning violence committed in the past?

*

Before leaving Canada, I'd read of the infamous 186 uneven steps inmates had to climb carrying massive chunks of rock out of the quarry, and of the Dutch Jews who committed suicide by holding hands and jumping into it, but on the day I went to Mauthausen, it was very hot, stifling, and the air was filled with mosquito-chasing swallows who nested in the barracks. At the bottom of the quarry, there was still dew on the grass, and at the base of a cliff, a small pond contained fish with light-red fins. At what point in the quarry's history did fish first appear in this pond? There was a bird nearby that sounded like, but couldn't have been, an oriole. Climbing the renovated steps, I noticed numerous ants, their nests safely hidden beneath the worn, rippled stone.

Some of the barracks have been converted to a museum. That passing time keeps obliterating what occurred in this place seems to exonerate the millions of individual violent acts that once were inflicted here with an anarchic disregard:

Heinrich Himmler (2nd from right) with adjutants, 1941.jpg

---

18   In *The Fragility of Empathy After the Holocaust*, Carolyn J. Dean writes: "when there are calamities in Japan, says Rousseau, he can't get very worked up about them."

A corroded searchlight used at some point during the camp's existence points out a window that has the silhouette of a bird on it so present-day swallows don't fly into the glass. And in a room in which medical experiments took place, two visitors on 24.3.2013 left their names in magic marker on the wall and recorded that they found themselves "a bit cold" on their visit. Why did it occur to Chip and Yana to leave traces of themselves and their reaction to the weather on these walls that surround a dissecting table, and what did they think when they went underground to the memorial *Room of Names*, where the names of over 81,000 victims are gathered?[19]

Outside of the enormous gates—built by the inmates—and overlooking the quarry is a statue of a seated, bereft woman and lines from Brecht's poem "*O Deutschland Bleiche Mutter*" inscribed in the stone wall nearby some oversized, sculpted barb wire. That stone was fashioned first to inflict pain and then to commemorate it seems inevitably and stupidly ironic. Igneous rock: human grief: oblivion. As seconds passed during the 1940s, the present must have been enormous and dense with viciousness; but those individual moments have each vanished, been smoothed away into the open spaces sightseers amble through in the present. Space must have felt different then, too, with so much of it a suffocating extension of someone's flayed nerves, though in the barracks today one species has seen fit to communicate the danger of glass (melted silica as a protracted form of time) to another species with silhouettes, as though to say:

Schwalben
diese Fenster sind gefährlich;
fliegt nicht in sie hinein!

Swallows
these windows are dangerous;
don't fly into them!

---

19   If my writing about Mauthausen resembles this graffiti (down to my mentioning the weather), it doesn't deface the barracks; neither does it insist that it must be viewed by future visitors to the memorial site.

What can be said about individual deaths after they happen, what can be noticed about these newly made things, these suddenly useless bodies? Two men die violently: Franz Ziereis, Mauthausen's strapping commandant, in 1945, and an anonymous, gaunt Russian prisoner thrown into the quarry, whose only remaining trace is an undated photograph—but neither fatality has anything in common. If time could be retraced to those moments that separately comprised the years in which the camp existed, what would be released? Is there a kind of dormancy in events once lived?

Imagine a cook in one of Mauthausen's kitchens, his fingers smelling of potatoes. He might have made a gruel that fed René Gille, a survivor who reports that, after he'd descended into the quarry, it was terrible to be reminded of a scene from *Metropolis* "transposed from the screen to real life," adding that "all of the comrades who had seen the film … felt the same way." All of these lived intensities are gone from the camp that's now a memorial, though the movie's instantly available on the Internet. After reading Gille's evocations of Lang, I searched YouTube for the Moloch scene, and then felt an uncanny disgust as I watched the clip. I could see why Gille made the comparison. And at the same time, I couldn't help but wonder whether this was one of the first recorded instances of someone comparing active trauma to a movie they'd seen previously in a theatre. In the same book, a Dr. Milo Vitek describes an SS massacre of inmates so that "future generations will not forget." But we *have* forgotten: the faith victims placed in future remembrance, which was connected to the early twentieth century's anxious, utopian politics, has proven misplaced. Futile. I cannot imagine it otherwise. Too few of the perpetrators were punished. Human venality and the urgency of postwar politics ensured that what happened in the camps was barely recognized, and the desire of individuals to be remembered is incommensurate with the nullifying effects of time and the widespread ignorance of those with no experience of totalitarian violence. And there's no way of knowing how Vitek would judge the strangers wandering around these grounds nearly a century later, cameras at the ready—whether he'd observe us with approval, or incomprehension, or something else entirely. What is clear is that Himmler would have been both alarmed and incensed if he could have known what would happen to his prized *Konzentrationslager*.

*

To ponder the mystery of anguish, commemoration, and oblivion, the sense of impotence one feels when visiting such sites—no pain is relieved, no justice served by our presence there as tourists—I try to imagine the specificity of senseless suffering and place it against Marina Abramović's generous performance piece *The Artist is Present*, in which she sat in silence for seven hours a day from March 14 to May 31, 2010, at MoMA, allowing 1,545 visitors to sit across from her as she took in their faces for a few long minutes at a time, sitting for a total of 736 ½ hours. In those hours, she provided those across from her the certainty that they had been seen at least once in their lives, perhaps even recognized, in a shared and unthreatening gaze, a gift that is very rare, something that would never have been bestowed by the Nazis.[20] The visitor to Mauthausen obviously cannot act like Abramović and share a mutual presence with those who have vanished.

*

Following the more than a dozen birds Bruegel placed in the painting to create a clock-wise motion, one eventually notices that, off in the distance, a chimney fire has started: perhaps Auden is right; for Bruegel, a painting offers a dialectic in which danger and strife accompany beauty. *Hunters in the Snow* holds much of what makes up human experience: nature (both immediate and in the distant mountains, an imagined sublime), work, play, living alongside animals, what's involved in teaching children how to do something that's new to them. And always attentive to change, the painting intimates how time makes everything disappear: the dead fox over the centre hunter's shoulder must have left some blood on snow that's missing from view. It was when I noticed the pattern of threes—there are three descending hunters amidst three prominent trees—that I began to understand that Bruegel uses this pattern to rebuff the human capacity to make reality cohere. We sense that, for Bruegel, perceiving patterns is largely provisional: the third tree leads to a fourth that leads to yet another, but the viewer's eye initially perceives that threes dominate.[21] However, it's when two of the men's spears meet to make an isosceles triangle that things get complicated. The painting's triangle is a microcosm of artistic unity; intelligible form becomes a place

---

20   The Nazi gaze is apparent in Mer Targarona's 2018 movie *The Photographer of Mauthausen* when the camp's SS photographer looks at a picture he's taken of inmates: "I like it very much. It reminds me of Pieter Bruegel," a pernicious comparison.

21   This configuration is repeated with the sections of frozen water, though more thoroughly: the pond on which people are skating is divided into three parts, but this water meets a river that segues to the sea.

to reside amidst flux, becomes a moment's nest, but this arrangement is ephemeral, lasting for less than a second, because form in this painting is a mirage. This triangle can only be perceived from the viewer's vantage point—if the child in the nearby cluster of people by the inn turned to look at the hunters, she wouldn't see the spears meet the way we do— and the next second, when the men breathe in more cold air and take another step through the snow, the convergence of visual unity and the artistic urge to condense something of totality must disengage, leaving only disparate events and sensations. As the men move down the hill and we leave the painting, we're each returned to our place within historical time. Form is ultimately a momentary convergence of the fragmentary, nothing more.

*

Berger defines *happiness* as when the gift of well-being coincides with the gift of what exists; and for him, aesthetic experience "is the purest expression of this equation." Except for very rare occasions, I've hardly ever felt more joy or a more powerful sense of freedom than when I abandoned myself to peer into this huge painting that was so close to where I was standing. What my mind recoils against, though, is that the misery that was Mauthausen between 1938-1945 existed only a short journey from Bruegel's painting. I imagine looking at Bruegel's painting in the early 1940s, and then going to Mauthausen and peering into the quarry the same day. (I hired a driver, a student from Hungary, for the two-and-a-half–hour trip; there are reports of inmates making the journey from Vienna to the camp on foot.) In both instances, the visual act of overlooking a vast scene containing much human activity below would involve attentiveness and patience to take everything in, but then the comparison breaks down. Bruegel's painting returns the viewer's gaze, invites us to appreciate its formal and existential proper- ties, say to ourselves, yes, this is the way a curious, skillfully observant, and magnanimous mind might interrogate the various intersections of life and death occurring on a winter's day. Everywhere it says: each of us, we are part of what constitutes the world's *now*. The painting insists upon no hierarchy: the viewer's eye is encouraged to roam freely, whereas the violence in the quarry sprang from an oppressively hierarchical sys- tem built upon menace, misery, hatred, and stupidity. But the suffering that took place in Mauthausen castigates my thought experiment. A well-meaning abstraction conducted in the shelter of the imagination, it risks obscuring the pain that happened there. What *should have occurred* when I imagined viewing both Bruegel and the camp in the same afternoon is that my mind ought to have refused to perform the second part of the experiment: go up the hill from the village called Mauthausen to where the camp is.[22] If I can consent to beauty in the Bruegel, welcome it inside me, allow myself to then suppose that the world is good (though to do so, I must ignore how the fox experienced its death from the hunters, and then also the hunters' poverty), I can't perform the corollary of consenting to Mauthausen. And when I recognize that I must allow this violent suffering into my worldview, accept it with the same openness I do the Bruegel, I find myself almost immediately disavowing this knowledge. However, my inability to make this grim juxtaposition coexist also seems false somehow, perhaps even cowardly: I must not simply acknowledge Mauthausen, but I must also make its horror part of me to the same degree that I permit myself the joy of viewing Bruegel's painting. But this is impossible. Moreover, whether someone who didn't experience the camps could open him or herself even slightly to what happened there is irresolvable.

*

Hegel is especially useful to thinking about this problem when he says that "the life of the Spirit is not the life that shrinks from death… but rather the life that endures and maintains itself in it…. This tarrying with the negative is the magic power that converts it into being." If I agree that Spirit mustn't shrink from acknowledging death,[23] what I can't do is follow through and dialectically convert the Negative into a greater complexity of Spirit. I get stalled. I don't understand how to accomplish

---

22 An inmate of the camp, Marcel Faure, notes that Mozart, travelling on a barge along the Danube as a child, visited Mauthausen when it was only a village. Calling attention to the way Mozart "was bullied by the imbecile whims of the princeling [*sic*] Archbishop of Salzburg," Faure claims that the "fate Mozart endured binds him to the deportee in profound revery [*sic*]." How can the world exhibit itself in such a precise manner—a day in the child Mozart's life—moving within ongoing time and the unimaginable magnitude of what time erases into nothingness? Similarly confused by temporality, Adam Zagajewski notices that January 27th is both Mozart's birthday and the day when Auschwitz was liberated; to him, keeping these facts in mind, we must "live in a doubleness, in difficult, impossible doubleness."

23 Though Freud denies we can acknowledge our mortality: "We cannot, indeed, imagine our own death; whenever we try to do so we find that we survive ourselves as spectators."

what Hegel advises. Further, what does it mean to *understand* something? The word is slippery. There's a joyful click that occurs in the mind when one recognizes the meaning of words in another language, or, for that matter, when one comprehends Hegel's point about "tarrying with the negative." Are these instances of understanding? Yes... but. The nature of understanding also includes something rogue: the word exists on a wide, wide continuum, and we tend to recognize only parts of it. Here's a precise example of what I mean: one New Year's Day, the *New York Times* reprinted the "most-read" stories from the previous year, creating a kind of secular Zeitgeist; one article concerned a woman who was unintentionally killed because of a dispute between drug dealers. The mother of the dead woman says: "I don't think anyone can understand this pain unless they've gone through it themselves." If one accepts the accuracy of what this woman says (though of course only the sense, not the content, unless the reader has lost a child to violence), how is it possible, then, that the reporter can maintain in his Foreword that he deliberately "set out *to understand* [the woman's] pain" (emphasis mine)? It's as though he didn't hear what she was saying, despite choosing to quote her. What, then, does the word *understand* really entail? What would it mean to say that one can *understand* the beauty of Bruegel's painting? Or understand Mauthausen's innumerable acts of ferocity?

When I turn to etymology, I learn that *understand* derives from Old English *forstandan*, a word which locates thinking about something to standing nearby so as to observe it better. The notion of witnessing seems to form part of the background to the word, or perhaps even what's involved in basic recognition, as I recognize that it's raining and that this rain is needed to alleviate the drought the prairies experienced during the summer. There's much more to this urge to stand close to the Bruegel or to the quarry at Mauthausen than the need to acquire personal experience of an abstraction, however valuable this may be: what's at stake involves the drive to approach finitude, to discern its outlines, to move closer, and then to touch it. One person stands nearby a painting that another person's very specific hand crafted centuries before. In this finitude, there are inevitable constraints: one can return to *Hunters in the Snow* only a fixed number of times, and only once did I choose to grip with my hands the damp handles of the rust-coloured, surprisingly heavy corpse carrier in Mauthausen's crematorium—knowing that, as I did so, I was intruding upon the innumerable times that prisoners held the same handles when the carrier was a tool, not a relic.

It's as though what we try to understand gazes back and peers through us to something else. Brueghel's painting engages us as mortal creatures whose eyes take in the immensity beyond our bodies; standing in front of the work, we are transfixed, even compelled by the mystery, the endless forms finitude can take. Motion, colour, and physical need—each phenomenon addresses us in our individual sense of what they mean and how they occur. I cannot offer a corollary for Mauthausen, cannot say what Mauthausen initiates, except that what was taken out of the quarry wasn't simply painfully heavy blocks of stone: it's as though an infinite void was cut out of whatever made the present *present* during the exact minutes when the camp functioned. Familiarizing ourselves with historical data, spending most of a day walking on the camp's grounds, we are left to our inability to comprehend the endless particulars this place inflicted upon all who entered its stone gates. And yet, as Georges Didi-Huberman argues regarding Auschwitz, we are obligated to imagine, and doing so, "you never stop protesting against this history."

When I say that there's a drive to "touch" finitude, I mean that one wants to begin a journey from an abstract familiarity with something to a closer approximation with it, even though one knows that one can never reach the degree of immersion one seeks. To travel to Zurich in 2014 (as Steve did) in order to observe the Bollingen Tower, mindful that Jung's eyes once perceived the same building, is to transform what had been a hazy mental image into something more exact. That only Jung could recognize the building the way he himself did over the years is less important than the process which replaced a virtual image in Steve's mind with the singular particularity of the building. There's something deeply uncanny about this experience. (Though to be sure, reading *itself* is uncanny as one filters the unknown through what's familiar.) Because reading seems to involve multiple hermeneutic and imaginative acts, it engages several parts of the mind simultaneously. And at some level, there's always one recalcitrant, almost solipsistic, strand of the self that is skeptical of the ontological validity of what one reads, and this part, upon seeing the Bollingen Tower for instance, then might admit with a kind of benighted amazement, "So, it's really true, Jung and Zurich actually do exist."[24] Different from the untethered imagination that

---

24   I purchased Freud's *The Future of an Illusion* at the Freud museum that day, having had to sell my previous copy when I was broke as a student. Jung would find this synchronicity amusing; in the book, Freud notes: "It was as a grown-up man that I first stood on the hill of the Athenian acropolis… . Mingled with my happiness was a sense of astonishment that came to me as: so, it really is true, what we were taught at school. How shallow, how feeble must have been the belief I had acquired then in the actual

turns black marks on a page into images and sensations, this precise finitude then extends to the observer "standing" alongside it.[25] But I think the fundamental interaction that takes place in this contiguity is that one wishes to see and be seen simultaneously, even if one isn't conscious of this desire—which, depending upon a kind of magical thinking, also seeks existential awareness. Possibly part of Steve wanted to be seen by Jung in order to complicate his own finitude.

If Steve wished to be seen by Jung in Zurich and I subconsciously wanted the same from Hillesum in Amsterdam, this doesn't explain why anyone would go to a place like Mauthausen. Who would desire to stand in the quarry and be seen by what happened there? Unless some part of my mind believed that Mauthausen retains the power of the sublime, and I wished to get close to it without danger of being physically harmed. Is there, then, an implicit egoism, or worse, something akin to voyeurism, involved in wanting to understand something? Maybe. But it's also true that to desire to understand something is to move beyond the self, to turn toward something that has suddenly called out to us, something that we can sense without being immediately capable of acknowledging what it is.

When British soldiers liberated concentration camp inmates, Robert Antelme observes in *The Human Race*, they seemed to take in the prisoners' plights fairly quickly: "Most consciences are satisfied quickly enough, and need only a few words to reach a definite opinion of the unknowable.... *Unimaginable*: a word that doesn't divide, doesn't restrict. The most convenient word. When you walk around with this word as your shield, this word for emptiness, your step becomes more assured, more resolute, your conscience pulls itself together."

Distinguishing understanding from "having correct information and scientific knowledge," Hannah Arendt maintains that understanding requires "unending activity by which, in constant change and variation, we come to terms with and reconcile ourselves to reality, that is, try to be at home in the world." Arendt is surely correct to note that seeking to understand something necessitates the ceaseless "activity" of returning

---

truth of what I was being told for me to feel such surprise now!"

25   "Standing" implies both physical and mental contiguity. That is, to read Rilke's *Letters to a Young Poet* alongside Hillesum's diary is to observe how she transformed specific passages from her reading of Rilke into her own writing. This proximity to her thought is parallel to walking to an intersection in Amsterdam and then standing there because she recorded in her diary how she stopped at that precise location and got off her bike so she could jot down an idea that had just occurred to her.

to stand near what we're trying to comprehend, but how can anyone become "reconciled" with reality? What could be involved in the effort required to be "at home in the world"? And yet one keeps returning to what's at the source of one's perplexity. Perhaps, though, one should admit—openly and with humility—that there are some domains of human experience that require attention but are closed to anyone who hasn't undergone them personally. The day after I spoke with Steve I went to Amsterdam, partially to stand outside Hillesum's wartime residence of 6 Gabriël Metsustraat, stand there and try to imagine her leaving that very door to enter what now is called the Museumplein. *Forstandan.* And to fail once again in my efforts to eradicate the present, though Arendt believes that imagination is integral to understanding. For her, "imagination [is necessary] to take our bearings in the world," adding, "it is the only inner compass we have." If trying to imagine Hillesum's world must repeatedly fail, this failure can be extended to suggest the extraordinary difficulty of grasping what it could possibly mean to be anyone's contemporary.

Coda

Parmigianino's painting *Self-Portrait in a Convex Mirror* is down the hall from the room devoted to Bruegel. John Ashbery wrote his poem of the same title after visiting the Kunsthistoriche Museum in 1959. Attempting to negotiate the different ontologies of the present as manifested within Parmigianino's painting versus that of the onlooker in 1959, the poem offers that eventually the viewer is expelled from the painting's world because "You can't live there." If museums have closing times and at day's end thrust their visitors back into an ordinary itinerary, it's also true that an individual life can never be long, rich, or thoughtful enough to engage satisfactorily with *Hunters in the Snow*. As the painting shows, time, for us, necessitates motion, whether we trudge home after an exhausting day, glide on skates beneath a mountain, or step into whatever moment constitutes time as a visitor to Vienna on a particular day.

After leaving the Bruegel gallery, crossing Vienna's Ring, I found myself in the tropically humid and Art Nouveau *Schmetterlinghaus*, the Imperial *Butterfly House,* and eventually made my way to the Freud Museum at Bergasse 19, where he lived, consulted, and wrote. A huge pink sign indicates its location, the flamboyant sign as unexpected (considering Viennese propriety) as the Pope might be were he to bless a crowd with an animal made from a coloured balloon. The apartment is mostly empty, though one room has some roped-off period furniture and the original wallpaper. An exhibit containing Freud's tortoiseshell glasses and one of his fountain pens, uncapped and mute for decades, is a spot-on memorial to the man and his insights, a visual poem that elicits in perfect counterpoint the vanished guests who once frequented his weekly salons—among them, Lou Andreas-Salomé. What did she think as she participated in the conversation, when everyone must have known how close she'd been to Nietzsche and Rilke?

*

Not far from Freud's residence, a Roma woman sat silently in the hot, hot sun, hugging her knees up against her chest. While she was begging, she leaned against a wall of white stone that shimmered in the dry, otiose heat. Over two hours had passed since I'd first seen her but as I made my way back to the hotel, there she was, silent and motionless still… several lifetimes apart from where Freud had once studied and slept, held consultations with patients amidst the aura of his private and now invisible *Wunderkammer*. One would think I could remember, but I can't recall for certain whether I gave her a Euro or only noted her presence and kept walking, thinking of the early-morning flight that would take me the next day to Amsterdam's Schiphol airport, an immensity of activity there except along a gateway where the bouquets of flowers commemorating those lost on Malaysia Airline Flight 117 continued to pile up. Seeing them for the final time, I wondered when they would be taken away and the gateway restored to its original purpose.

INTERLUDE: THE VARIOUS
SPECIES OF TIME

I was thinking about what it would be like to live somewhere [as beautiful as Capri]. Would it fix my brain?

—Jenny Offill, *Dept. of Speculation*

Fastening the lens cap back on my camera, I noticed three men making their way on the crowded sidewalk: a young man in handcuffs escorted by two cops. One of them met my gaze, only to challenge it. Inside the shopping bag between my feet was a carving of a northern flicker wrapped up in paper. I'd just bought it to give as a joke to my friend Kelly, a man whom I've known since childhood, because one had been boring into the siding on his house in Calgary all that summer. This busy street was in the small town of Canmore in the Rockies; the carving was a life-sized male meant to be a door knocker; and clouds were spilling over the nearby mountain range called Three Sisters. I'd taken their picture because the clouds looked like they were turning the peaks into barely visible islands, or perhaps the rocks in a Zen garden in Kyoto. But the black-and-white print on the wall behind me today differs from what I saw several years ago in the camera's viewfinder, showing my memory to be off: today the clouds resemble the spray of waves breaking on a rocky coast. Always, always, always, the endless patter of mental associations that obscure the chaotic simplicity of walking awkwardly with your arms pinioned behind your back.

*

Apart from being a tourist destination, Canmore has nothing in common with Prague, yet the two are inseparable for me because when I first learned the names of these mountains I couldn't help recalling a photograph of Kafka's three sisters taken in 1898. The connection was the verbal echo, though the huge, bleached-white nineteenth-century collars on the three little girls in the studio portrait likely resemble the nuns' habits of which Albert Rogers was reminded when he woke up after a storm and saw the snow-covered peaks above Canmore in 1883. He originally called the mountains the Three Nuns, but the name's subsequently been amended. (Rogers thought that the name was altered because it then became more safely Protestant, a nicely subdued jab at local propriety.) Because Kafka's sisters were each killed in the Holocaust, the carefully posed children, their three floral bouquets, and their refusal to look at the photographer all make the photograph unsettling. Knowing that these children grew into women who were murdered by the Nazis means, however, that we can't see the picture solely as a portrait that presumably decorated one of the Kafka apartments. My linking these mountains with the family photograph taken in Prague is spurious. Unsavory. And yet, making mental connections is inevitable and instantaneous: the mind can't help exhibiting its memory.

What concerns me about this process is the innate subjectivity, the underlying egoism, that necessarily underlies associative thinking. Whether I was the only person on the street that day who envisioned Kafka's sisters upon viewing the mountain range isn't my point; rather, I dislike and mistrust how we tend to take our everyday experience to be normative, when it's much more likely that it's atypical. We continuously suppose that what we perceive is shared by others and that we participate in what David R. Loy calls "consensus reality." But this is to immediately disregard how our own idiosyncratic memories partially constitute our experience of the present, intruding upon and disrupting what our various senses take in at the time. If there's a kind of smooth arrogance which nudges us to believe that our own experience resembles that of other people, it also never fails to astonish me how alone we are, even in ordinary life, and how we aren't more perplexed by this basic isolation.

Managing the Anxiety Generated by NLD
It is often impossible to appreciate the level of the child's anxiety, given the child's outward, masked appearance. In our experience, most children with NLD live with chronic fears that pervade their lives. They take those feelings for granted, not realizing that most people do not feel the same way.

Joseph Palombo, *Nonverbal Learning Disabilities: A Clinical Perspective*

As the man in custody was guided toward the police car just off Main Street, did it occur to him that he couldn't have envisioned—when he last woke up in his own bed—that this particular afternoon would assemble itself in the humiliating way it did? How long did the bystanders ambling past restaurants and shops keep in mind that something slightly unusual was happening in their midst? How long would it take before the barely concealed immediacy of their own lives closed over that chaotic moment they saw of the young man's day, his difficulties as inconsequential as a stone tossed into the nearby Bow River?

My family visits Canmore frequently, often using the town as a base to go hiking in the Kananaskis region. But I always try to spend some solo time walking along the Bow River, wondering how best to describe its fading jade colour, all the while looking for the scattering juncos, magpies, and the occasional red-tailed hawk that live there. Unlike the trees, whose needles barely move in the wind, the Bow, carved in another time, is always going fast, always altering what it is. I can see why such a river could be identified as a god, and if it too easily reminds me of writing a diary—you can never keep up with what has happened—I sense how the comparison of a river to passing time misses the utter plenitude of what happens all around us.

*

From Pirsig's *Zen and the Art of Motorcycle Maintenance*:

> All the time we are aware of millions of things around us—these changing shapes, these burning hills, the sound of the engine, the feel of the throttle, each rock and reed and fence-post and piece of debris beside the road—aware of these things but not really conscious of them unless there is something unusual or unless they

reflect something we are predisposed to see…. We take a handful of sand from the endless landscape of awareness around us and call the handful of sand the world.

*

In *Spectral Evidence: The Photography of Trauma*, Ulrich Baer contests the traditional "model of time-as-river" by setting it against its "counterpart… the Democritean conception of the world as occurring in bursts and explosions, as the rainfall of reality [which] privileges the moment rather than the story, the event rather than the unfolding, particularity rather than generality."

*

Perhaps because of the current, the river's perfect for skipping stones. The day before I bought the flicker, my wife Amy and two sons (Jakob and his older half brother, Jesse, from my first marriage) and I had been skipping stones near the abandoned railroad bridge, but unfortunately, not long after we started playing, someone walking her dog warned us of recent cougar sightings, so we needed to leave.

It's a bit hard to imagine Hegel skipping stones, but he does refer to children throwing stones into a river as a demonstration of how it is our nature to alter objects external to ourselves and thereby recognize who we are. Living near rivers for much of his life, perhaps he'd simply observed children at play, but it's much more fun to imagine Hegel competing with Hölderlin and Schelling, when they roomed together in Tübingen, each trying to beat the other to see whose side-arm was most skillful. If this trio of buddies did indulge themselves in skipping stones, Hegel would note that they were doing something entirely marvelous. Ruminating on play, he would decide that the self-conscious desire to have an effect on the world is the basis for all art. And if we could give him a cell phone, perhaps even Hegel would consider taking a selfie with his friends, the Neckar River in the background.

*

I've never really felt at home anywhere I've lived, and have often wondered what it's like for people who spend their lives in places the rest of us only visit as tourists. What would it mean to have a place like Canmore or a European capital as an anchor to your life? Once, trying to make conversation with a cab driver (who was taking me early one morning to Prague's train station), I casually complimented him on his city, telling him that it was beautiful. "It is for you," he answered, looking at me in the rearview mirror, watching me as I was put in my place. When I saw him looking at me in this way, I wished I could remember his life the way he did, and also know what had brought him to this insignificant moment, driving a customer to the train station downtown, someone heading for Berlin early on Wednesday, November 9, 2011.

There are so many ways time can be constituted: time spent shopping; time in handcuffs; the time inside a starving cougar; carving birds to make some money; watching Kelly, my childhood friend, eventually raise a family with Patti, one of my sisters. Two photographs of Three Sisters, one taken in Canmore of mountains, the other 113 years earlier in Prague, the family portrait holding what it means to be looked at by a stranger alongside the enigma of flesh. Or, the time inside a flat river stone held in a boy's hand that's then side-armed across glacial meltwater. Reading Hegel's *Lectures on Fine Art*. An unshaven Czech driving a tourist who speaks only English in a cab on Wednesday, a few kilometers from Kafka's grave, Kafka who is buried with his parents and who hated, absolutely hated Prague—or *Prag*, as he would have called it.

Or, time as an elliptical anniversary: November 9th as the bizarre date that links *Kristallnacht* with the fall of the Berlin Wall. How to imagine 3 different subjective experiences of time?

—Benjamin Murmelstein, the chief rabbi of Vienna, on November 9, 1938 (*Kristallnacht*), encountering a gleeful Adolf Eichmann in the widespread violence.

—Angela Merkel on November 9, 1989 (the date the Berlin Wall fell), long before she became German Chancellor; Murmelstein had died on October 27 of that year.

—Angela Merkel on December 19, 2016 (the date of a truck attack on Berlin's *Breitscheldplatz*), which would become a private anniversary, mostly for the families of the victims.

*

With Ha Ling Peak as a backdrop, Canmore's secondhand bookstore was destroyed by Alberta's severe flooding in the spring of 2013. Located below street level (next door to a candy shop that still remains), it was always surprisingly well-stocked. On a visit with Jesse two years before the flood, I found a collection of Zola's photographs, Frederick Karl's controversial Kafka biography[26], and best of all, Tillie Olsen's *Tell Me a Riddle*, the latter signed by the author with an inscription to a Canmore resident who seemed to have kept it for more than twenty years before selling it. There, in handwriting so small that it almost takes a magnifying glass to read, Olsen wrote:

To _____ _____:

"These things shall be" (p110-11)
Your face [something crossed out] *and beautiful—*
Thank you for your listening tonight.
May the best be for you
Tillie Olsen

May 1990

When I read the inscription, I was initially concerned that the book had been part of an estate sale—why would anyone who'd met Olsen part with it?—but a Google search referred to a recent public event attended by the original owner. Whatever the reason the book was sold, it became mine for four dollars. I wasn't there for the Olsen reading—although it's unclear where it took place—because I was a student in 1990, living a long way from Alberta. It was around then that I first read "Tell Me a Riddle" in an anthology. I've subsequently reread the story maybe twenty times, taught it when I could, and each time, its final lines induce tears. No other piece of writing, however moving—indeed, no other work of art—has consistently affected me this way. This particular short story seems to engage in a kind of emotional alchemy that I've no desire to scrutinize too closely, and this bit of fraying ink (written no doubt in haste with its crossed-out passage) is in itself of complicated worth. The story compresses much of what mattered in the twentieth century. Olsen

---

26   Michael André Bernstein rejects Karl's notion of "Kafka-as-prophet of Nazism," but more important, finds the biography's tone of "moral scrupulousness" to be off-putting given that Karl dedicates the book "to the 6 million, Europeans murdered by Europeans." Bernstein argues: "there is the more serious question of how the biography of even the most brilliant modern Jewish writer could possibly serve as a fitting memorial to the victims of the Shoah. The disproportion between the offering and what is being commemorated is so great that it approaches the grotesque."

would definitely have maintained that the book counts more than her signature does, and I'm also certain that she would have turned the story into ash… instantly… (would even had denied herself the joy of writing it) if only the utopian desires it expresses could be fulfilled. What gives this material object its value to me, though, derives from that entirely unexpected encounter with Olsen. The moment I read her signature, the other parts of that August day suddenly seemed distant. The question of whether Jesse and I should go hiking in the mountains later that morning, given the increasingly overcast cloud cover, lost its immediacy. I'd known that Olsen had died a few years before I opened the slightly battered paperback in the store, but the fact of her death suddenly felt nearby, as close to me as the store's wooden floor. Looking at the dedication, I became detached from where I was: the day seemed to be elsewhere, was somehow taking place upstairs and across the street. And at the same time, that minuscule handwriting—startling, yet strangely reassuring—was uncanny, as it made the world's strangeness appear in a way it never had before.

*

Only a little before he was condemned to prison for slandering the French army regarding the Dreyfus Trial, Zola took a picture of his family with Jeanne Rozerot having lunch. Accompanying the image in the book I bought along with the Olsen paperback, Zola's daughter Denise is quoted, recalling her father as an indulgent parent who never punished his children. She then adds that another memory from her childhood concerned a parrot that had been given to her father by a friend who had a brother (as she puts it) "in the colonies." This parrot was greedy and mean, often biting Zola's fingers as he "put bits of banana in between the bars of the cage." To avoid imprisonment by the French authorities, Zola fled to England with his family. While in England, he liked to take photos while riding his bicycle. Denise became a writer, living from September 20, 1889, to December 31, 1942. She was born and died in Paris. The existence of the Nazi death camps was first made public in the British parliament two weeks before her death.

THE FLÂNEUR, AMSTERDAM, AND A HAWK

Sunday, July 27, 2014

A woman startled up the street ahead of me, reeling away from a storefront, colliding into the man alongside her. Her peripheral vision had suddenly alerted her to a cobra. Attached to a wire, the creature was displayed behind a toy-shop window, rising up and then recoiling down. She must have seen it when it had been at its height. Because Jakob was obsessed with snakes that year, I bought him a cobra stuffy, barely fitting it into my backpack. It nestled there for the rest of the day, along with a book and an acrylic reproduction of Jan Steen's *The Burgher of Delft and His Daughter*. A few canals before I bought the cobra, I saw a man gesturing, then knocking on a full-length window in Amsterdam's Red-Light District. He was greeted by someone dressed as a geisha in the door alongside the window, one of many such windows nearby where Rembrandt once had his studio. It looked as though the two of them might have been close together in age.

Walking in large cities makes me attentive to the body. And to how abstractions assume corporeality. The toy cobra seemed to have instantly summoned some primordial fear that jolted that woman from her sense of herself walking down a street, her body instantly flooded with cortisol. Because several years have passed since I noticed her encounter with the snake, I wonder whether her scare has been forgotten or if it's part of the repertoire she shares with the person with whom she was walking. From another direction, this one also involving a body quickening with hormones: how are minutes measured when spent in a twenty-first–century brothel? For the woman? Her customer? Is fucking subject to history? Would their transaction be largely the same as one that took place in the seventeenth century, or was it affected by Internet pornography? And wouldn't it be more accurate to say that the person who appeared as a geisha was a sex worker who'd metamorphosed into a courtesan for her clients' imagination?

Because I'd recently seen the Jeff Wall exhibit at the Stedelijk, I could envision the busy street scene passing for one of his tableaux were it not for the actual condom that presumably was opened by someone's fingers. I could sense the photograph's necessary drizzle. Leaving the hotel that Sunday morning, I'd noticed that the Band-Aid neatly fallen on the sidewalk was still there after two nights of rain, the damp air holding the odors of hash smoke from the nearby beneath-the-street-level marijuana cafés.

*

What if for some people the most interesting thing they'll do with their bodies is grow older?

*

In *Rembrandt's Eyes*, Simon Schama lists some of the objects that the painter collected, among them coral, a Turkish powder horn, a giant's helmet, and Javanese shadow puppets, noting that this collection "reflected his instinctive, Aristotelian belief that from the infinitely pleasing *variety* of the world would appear, unforced, a revelation of the Creator's design."

*

Craving a solitude that nearly hums, a flâneur is another kind of collector. Every footstep widens what's visual. If I can't escape being a tourist, a flâneur woven from souvenirs and a digital camera, I can disappear into the privilege of anonymity. Details accumulate, and the self almost disappears. One eye going gonzo in slow motion. The other more detached, a bit of lake remembering the shore. Walking this way is hiking inside a series of detours. The surfaces upon which people walk or that awning protecting customers of the LGBTQ club, its name Reality, lit with pink and green neon, these surfaces alert the eye to the fact that everything encountered, everything—from the fallen Band-Aid to those standing in line outside of the Anne Frank Huis near the Homomonument, the triangular granite memorial built to commemorate gays and lesbians killed by the Nazis—everything has its own invisible history.

How can anyone learn to live inside what the eye can hold when everyone keeps vanishing? And yet, each of us retains certain details that persist for years, but why some over others? For me, the details that remain are those in which what's visible shimmers with what can't be seen directly. And these moments are littered opulently in the ongoing wreckage of time. These encounters are always unexpected, intimating how others, usually strangers, are deep within the experience of their own lives.

—Years ago, the words *I'm sorry* written with chalk on a sidewalk, and then again on the next concrete block, and again eighty more times. Someone must have bent down on a knee, apologizing repeatedly for something only the addressee could identify. Each word coming from a megaphone that only one person in the world could hear. And the writer knew the path this person would take.

—A blue and white bus with grills on its windows unloads convicts— the bus and the men belonging to the Sheriff of Cook County—and these men kid around, one of them grinning as he moons Andy and me, these men conscripted to clean up the trash left over from that year's gay pride parade in Chicago. On a Sunday—the chance to be on the open street and make a few bucks.

*

Something with which a flâneur must contend: there are innumerable ways of *not* being a flâneur: going to work, shopping for sex, fleeing as a refugee. Joining others in a demonstration. When Greta Thunberg said "we will not be bystanders" to a crowd in Montreal a few months ago, some of us in the prairies were stretched out on the ground protesting government inaction on climate change by playing dead in front of the provincial legislature. The sky not noticeably a different one from when I lay on a hill as a child. And yet, global warming is making it so.

If, for Baudelaire, the flâneur "is a kaleidoscope gifted with consciousness… an 'I' with an insatiable appetite for the 'non-I,'" then participants in political demonstrations have stern emotions welded to the moment. Chanting slogans creates a sensation halfway between work and defiance. When a counter-protestor told me that Jesus himself had instructed him to oppose the children's climate strike, that God had told him that global warming is a hoax, I felt fury, not the detachment that characterizes the flâneur. And later, it was impossible not to heckle the provincial environment minister who openly lied about his government's commitment to addressing climate change to the crowd of young people, including my son, a boy who long ago relinquished his collection of stuffies.

*

The first time I'd been in Amsterdam I was twelve, only three years older than Jakob is now. My father was a geography teacher and had brought us with him for a sabbatical. Somehow I still have the diary I kept: we visited the Anne Frank House on August 7, 1972. Likely influenced by something my parents said, I wrote "Ann's [sic] house not as bad as expected," though I've no idea as to what my parents had in mind, and I suspect that neither did they. (Perhaps they were concerned about the possibility of disturbing photographs such as those we'd seen earlier at Dachau.) Did it mean anything for them to see the marks on the wall that measured Anne and Margot's heights as they grew? Later that day, while my mother and sisters went to a miniature city in The Hague, I began reading *The Diary of a Young Girl*, unaware that it had been expurgated. What gives me pause now is that only thirty years separated my reading of her diary and Anne's starting it. And on August 7— the day we climbed the stairs to the annex—on that date in 1944 everyone in hiding had been arrested, soon to be sent north to the transit camp Westerbork and then deported to Poland. That no one can understand how August 7, 1944, can change into August 7, 1945, all the way to 1972, continuously destroys much of what we believe about living in the world.

According to my diary, our family ate spaghetti for dinner in an urban campground with filthy toilets. I don't know what else we could have done than proceed with our ordinary lives that evening, but numerous things perturb me now. We didn't know that Otto Frank was then living in Switzerland; if we had, it probably would have meant little to us. But it should have meant a great deal. Despite standing on floors where he and his family once stood, it never occurred to us that we lived in the same world Anne's father did. I think it's fair to say that a family like mine lacked the imagination to even *try* to envision a world in which Otto Frank lived. We were merely tourists. Because my father was interested in World War II, we'd gone to Normandy. And because the Holocaust was connected to this war, we'd visited the two sites commemorating Nazi victims most familiar to North Americans—Dachau and Anne Frank's House—but we were middle-class WASP Canadians: the Holocaust was terrible, of course, but it didn't have anything to do with us. We also blithely travelled through Spain, Portugal, and Greece, each a dictatorship then. I remember asking my parents about the omnipresent banners in Greece showing a soldier's silhouette in front of a phoenix amidst flames, but was reassured that the regime of the Colonels, once again, had nothing to do with us. It was only when I read Elaine Scarry's *The Body in Pain* that I gleaned any sense of what was being inflicted on people hidden away from Delphi's ruins or the beaches that we'd toured with our VW, a Canadian flag emblazoned on the leather protective cover for its spare tire, the tire affixed to the front of the van, announcing our nationality to everyone who saw us pass by.

I don't mean to sound ungrateful to my parents, but I wonder whether tourism teaches habits that persist long after you've returned home. Does the intensity of new experience give greater strength to the mental habits we create while passing through foreign countries? When traveling we had the sense of being exposed to astonishing things—no one from the small town in southern Ontario from which we came had been to these exotic places—and we also felt entirely *different* from the people who lived in those countries and didn't always speak English. I had no sense then not only of how ethically dangerous tourism can be, but also how it insulates people from reality just as much as I would later learn that a lifetime of alcohol abuse can. At what point does an uncomfortable fact—such as the Colonels' control over Greece—succeed in challenging the tourist's capacity for entertainment and novelty? From this distance now, it seems that we were too busy taking part in the generally hurried human sensibility that blends an overall insensitivity to others with the haphazard blindness we extend to ourselves. I didn't understand, then, that the excitement of going to new places can have unforeseen effects on subsequent ordinary life: we were back in Canada, my father to his teaching, my middle sister and I to school, when Black September killed Israeli athletes participating in that year's Olympics, only 36 years after Hitler's Olympics in Berlin. That we had been in Munich only weeks before meant that what connected us to Bavaria was our individual memories, my father's slide photographs, and the Haufbräuhaus beer stein he still keeps to decorate his bar. When we'd toured the Olympic village, the new structure ready to receive the world's athletes, it was beyond our imagination to permit the possibility that people could die there. And when we learned that it was so, we did what presumably most people watching their TVs did at the time: we ignored what was happening by refusing to acknowledge a reality that contains such violence.

One definition of flânerie: a state of mind in which the tourist's separation from local life is blended with the attempt to escape solipsism. And curiosity: attentive to details, the flâneur is buoyant with curiosity.

*

Ronnie Goldstein–van Cleef, then a teenager, met the Frank family at Westerbork and in 1998 recalled, "The Franks were pretty depressed. They had had the feeling that nothing could happen to them…. They always walked together." The last she saw of them was at Birkenau, when she encountered Mrs. Frank and her daughters. Anne and Margot were both suffering from scabies.

*

On her way to work several years ago, my wife befriended a woman who took the same bus. This woman, who grew up in Ceaucescu's Romania and then became a professor of Greek philosophy, invited us to dinner. While the table was being set, I looked at her bookcase. On the spine of one book a thumbnail photograph of a woman gazing into the camera faced the apartment. Its title, *Etty Hillesum: An Interrupted Life*, made me curious. It was my copy of this book that was in my backpack in Amsterdam, along with the cobra.

Hillesum wrote from 1941 to 1943, managing to embody the perplexities facing a young, ambitious writer who gradually came to understand that, as a Jewish woman living in Nazi-controlled Amsterdam, she was unlikely to survive. She wrote of her desire to "know this century of ours, inside and out… to run [her] fingers along the contours of our age." The question that won't go away is how these contours appeared when she was inside a cattle car going east into Poland. Having refused to go into hiding, she perished on November 30, 1943. No book has affected me more. Upon reading the first few pages, I recognized in her a sensibility that, more than any other I've encountered, mirrors my own (especially in her attempts to thwart depression). More importantly, the letters she wrote in great haste from Westerbork—the transit camp from where people were deported to the camps—are the quick summation of everything she knew and saw; following the Rilke of *Duino Elegies*, they are what she managed to show the angels, to alert them to what they (and we) needed to know. I reread this book often and take it with me when I visit places she'd been: standing outside her apartment at Gabriël Metsustraat 6 in Amsterdam; Westerbork; Auschwitz-Birkenau.

*

On November 28, 1941, heading to the apartment of her mentor and lover, Julius Spier, Hillesum suddenly got off her bicycle to record an observation in her notebook. Because I'd wanted to see places where I knew with certainty she'd been, I went to the corner of Apollolaan and Michelangelostraat, read the diary entry again, and then a man riding a bicycle while texting almost hit me as I crossed the street. A few minutes later I stood in the small landing outside the apartment in which Spier once lived and imagined Hillesum standing there, looking down the steps, perhaps waiting if it was raining, and then heading home.

*

Every day for centuries, people have wandered around these canal-lined streets, each of us making a separate blur through our lives: over time, who could possibly distinguish one human cloud from another? There were lineups outside the Van Gogh museum and the Anne Frank Huis, but no passersby paused over the memorial plaques along the walkway commemorating Nazi victims who once lived along the street beneath our feet. Having been given the address where the Jewish Council had its offices and been told there's a commemorative sign—I can't miss it—I walk to find only the number: 58 Nieuwe Keizersgracht. No sign. But a woman is sitting by the door at the top of the stairs. I ask her if she knows whether this is where the *Judenrat* once met. Yes, I think so, she says, there's a plaque or something. But we discover it's gone because—she suddenly remembers—the building's being repainted. They'll replace it when the job's done, she tells me. I thank her, walk down the street, and watch her get up from the steps and greet her friends. And then I return to take in what this building looks like without being able to see what's important: Hillesum and many others worked there unwillingly amidst the frantic uncertainty involved in trying to adapt to the shifting policies and escalating difficulties the Nazis inflicted upon the Jewish population. Today it's simply a street bordering a canal.

Then I notice a familiar bird near a barge in the canal. It's called a *Rode hals fuut* in Dutch; in English, the red-necked grebe. There it is, bobbing in the sway left by a motorboat, across from 58 Nieuwe Keizersgracht, a monogamous and migratory bird whose colours—rufous neck and yellowish beak—stretch from the Pleistocene → although she could see the Rijksmuseum from her bedroom window, Hillesum never mentions going inside, and so I don't know whether she ever looked at Steen's *The Burgher of Delft and His Daughter*. The painting depicts a woman along with her child appealing for alms to a finely dressed burgher. He doesn't meet her gaze; nor does his daughter, who seems intent on challenging viewers. Separate from the others in the painting, she's sauntering off to her day, leaving her home and its vase of flowers decorating a windowsill, a still life that Steen must have known was a masterpiece all on its own. This still life leads to the painting's technique of grafting together heterogeneous elements. The scene is an intricate study in realism that's also a moral fable, whose complexity derives from an implied narrative that's as multi-layered as the people's clothing in the painting. As interested in the varying textures offered by the physical world as in the intense psychology it provides, the painting combines several distinct ways of living in, and representing, the world. Obdurate and slightly worn masonry exists alongside the mystery of flesh. Vulnerability encounters thoughtful indifference, and the burgher's daughter separates herself from all of this. In her posture and her eyes, she communicates the past few years of her life, her experience having taught her to ignore her father so she can move towards whatever's coming in her direction, to step toward her future in her carefully audacious way.

As 1655—when the painting was completed—shifted into 1656, what got irrevocably left behind? It's as though there were strands of dense reality interwoven with the canvas's edges when Steen first showed it, and time abrades them to such an extent that viewers today are presented merely with a canvas held in its frame. What draws me to this painting is its seamless investigation into various modes of consciousness while embodying numerous disparate styles. Because painters can manage this multiplicity so openly, it's impossible not to envy them.

If Hillesum left no record indicating that she'd observed either this painting or others by Steen, a friend she'd made at Westerbork clearly had: the journalist Philip Mechanicus. In his diary, Mechanicus summons Steen when he describes people boarding a transport being sent to Poland:

> *Tuesday February 15 [1944]* The actual departure was, in the end, much more harrowing than we had all thought it would be…. In all the small squares of the window openings there are men and women crowded together… it is like a row of Jan Steen canvases placed side by side, but in a minor key…. The train slips away like a ghost; it glides past like a book with living pictures.

*

To Costica Bradatan, the "essay is an impossible genre. It seeks to capture not the things themselves, not even things in change, but change itself."[27] As I've been writing of Amsterdam,

I've been watching animals:

nuthatches,

fox squirrels, a rare

pileated woodpecker, and lately a hawk. Animals can't risk being flâneurs. What voices do their brains, their nervous systems give them—first person, second, or third? More likely, an agrammatical function that's hidden from us—

---

27   When I consider change, I'm mindful that July 27, 2014, would have been Lynn's and my 29th wedding anniversary.

Earlier this morning there were a heap of ashes in the snow by the old fence alongside the alley, but binoculars have shown the feathered

heap to be the remains of a feast. The sharp-shinned
hawk I glimpsed late yesterday and watched
for about twenty minutes must have eventually
made a kill. When the bird turned in
my direction, I could see the drill of a black pupil at the center of a tawny golden iris, the black the same as the hook ending its beak, and today, the pigeon's leftover agony is hardening in the snow, is becoming the brittle colour of a faded postage stamp in contrast to the fire-engine red of the two well-stocked birdfeeders that must have caught the hawk's attention—

CELL 23

Sunday, October 16, 2016

Each day, when the alarm wakes me, I immediately sense that there's something wrong. It takes a few minutes for the hard, jittery feeling of anxiety to recede. I brew a pot of coffee, take some vitamins, put some frozen fruit in a bowl to thaw for breakfast, and then read until Amy and Jakob wake up, usually for an hour and a half. On Saturday, October 15, it's been Maggie Nelson's *The Argonauts* for a few days:

> I am interested in offering up my experience and performing my particular manner of thinking, for whatever they are worth. I would also like to cop easily to my abundant privilege—except that the notion of privilege as something to which one could "easily cop," as in "cop to once and be done with," is ridiculous. Privilege *saturates*, privilege *structures*. [emphasis in original]

*

But when I wake today, Sunday, I'm not at home. I come to lying on a slab of what feels like concrete, and then everything slams into me: I got so utterly drunk last night that I threatened suicide and Amy called the police. I recall a huge man coming at me in our living room, others behind him—all moving in a mist—and a woman too? Yes, I can see her. And next: handcuffs. Shoving me into the back seat of a cruiser, they didn't place a hand on my head as they pushed me in, something I testily commented on. In the station, no, I didn't want a lawyer, no, fuck you: a psychiatrist. Don't any of you get this, I asked them? But now, it's the morning. Never has a Now felt like this: crushing. Swirled somehow. Crushing. Still drunk. My glasses are gone. No watch. The cell doesn't have bars for a door; instead, there's some type of thick, streaked plastic separating me from the corridor. A very small metal toilet with no lid. Someone calls out from another cell. A metal sink. No shoes or belt. My notebook where I always keep it

> inside my jacket pocket, but no pen. At least I have the cell to
> myself. Have I destroyed everything?
> Who *am* I?
> If. If I hadn't. If I'd stopped earlier, stopped
> drinking earlier that night
> and just gone home.

*

When I get out of here, my marriage will be dead, and how can I manage to end everything—end me—end everything for real? Various scenarios offer themselves, all dependent-on-being-able-to get away and be alone. If only I could be just a tree and pull my branches back into my trunk and then shrink back into something so small no one would ever know.

Still drunk, but I can't sleep. I try but stop myself because then I'll have to wake up here again. Time must be passing, but it refuses to take me with it. I want my brain to obey when I tell it to eat itself.

More noise, someone hollering to get out, and finally a cop walks by in the corridor and he tells me which city I'm in when I ask him, but he shrugs his shoulders when I want to know when I'll be allowed to go. Even though I can't see him clearly, I can feel his contempt as he takes me in his gaze and then tosses me aside.

I piss into the metal toilet and would give a lot for a coffee.

*

The cop's a Ketchup Mountie. Years ago when Andy and Jesse were kids, we were inside a Dairy Queen when a bunch of Mounties from the RCMP training centre came in, some with a red strip down a pant leg, others a yellow one. I identified them as Ketchup and Mustard Mounties… to this day my kids remember the designations. Eventually Ketchup Mountie comes by pushing a cart like those used by airline stewards. No coffee's available, I don't want a muffin, and then he kicks a can under the cell door so it spins into the cell. It's juice.

Any number of hours later, when I'm released into the corridor—after seeing no psychiatrist or anyone at all—I see the black numbers 23 on the door to the cell. The police officer, a young man with confident yet undernourished stubble, takes me to a room where I'm given my belongings and then walked up the stairs, shown a phone, and told I'll *be all right*. Bless him, I mean truly, because I feel lower than any kind of excrement and something lets me hate him, too. A piece of stiff paper has been attached to the bag of my things; much like a tag airlines use, it has my surname and cell number. I'd spent the night in Cell 23.

Eventually our white Prius shows up. It's raining and cold. Amy has sent Jakob to a friend's house so she and I can talk. Everything in my life depends on her. And I allow myself some contempt of my own: no one could kill themselves in a garage with a Prius, you middle-class asshole.

*

Reconstructing the past day, Saturday the fifteenth, is mostly simple. Got up early. Read some Proust, some Nelson, and then Franz Wright. Took our car to the garage to get snow tires put on. Raked leaves and then went hard on the exercise bike. Amy and Jakob were out for the afternoon, so I walked downtown to meet up with Gerry. Have known him since our first year of university, his girlfriend becoming friends with Cindy in an art history class they were taking. Gerry and I took a philosophy class together, and then more than 30 years passed. He's in Regina because of his job—he works for a company that invigilates exams like the ALSAT—and I keep buying more drinks. No woman in his life, and he hates his job. We talk about movies. New ones and those he introduced me to decades before. It's because of him that I admire Wim Wenders. I buy more and more, including several Jägermeister, which I do because I enjoyed drinking it in Paris one night. I want the feeling I got in Paris to return.

Patterns count.

*

Next, I'm not sure. But this is what I remember: Leaving a cab. Waking up on a lawn down the street from our house. No hat, no wallet. Then waking Amy, telling her I've been mugged. She spends time on the phone cancelling credit cards and I then go into the kitchen and fill up my suit coat with knives. She sees me, calls the police. I get up and pour myself a glass of tequila, telling her that I'm going to be incarcerated and so am having a final drink. Then there's noise at the front door and there's a crowd of huge people moving quickly toward me, especially the one leading; he seems to fill the room as he sweeps by the terrarium where Jakob's corn snake, Buddy Buttercup, is presumably sleeping. The cops don't put a hand on my head when they put me in the cruiser.

*

Turns out I hadn't been mugged. What likely happened is that I'd tripped on a curb, passed out, and when I woke, I couldn't find my black fedora or wallet in the dark. The neighbour down the street found my hat and wallet on his lawn, and then apparently returned everything in the morning while I was in jail. Inside the wallet was a receipt for $141.26. The time on the receipt was 00:03:58. Less than five minutes after midnight… and I woke Amy around 3:00, which means I had to have been passed out on the lawn for a few hours.

To Not Have Empty Space

around me.   Imagine. It's taken   a drift of
swollen   and immediately
vanished
          years upon decades

but drinking's toll   finally appeared
one prefigured ↔ yet unforeseen   October
night   it was   as

though a meat
thermometer suddenly
                        stabbed into

my left ear drum, bringing me
to my knees on a sidewalk

when I woke

in a blur on a concrete bench
inside a   wavery

jail Cell No. 23 and its grubby its sometimes hollering   communal
air   my glasses
missing   wallet and keys and leather belt gone too   and   the metal
                         point
of the thermometer (real
or otherwise)   kept

digging at my brain   that finite and invisible
home where words and booze and   memory   *once*

flourished un-
restrained and together they'd

greedily &   joyfully &   cunningly   combine
to bring
         something back

from the many kinds of   world nearby:

the tidal littoral zone   —an implicity of mebbe Basho imploding—
and render

its precise and fluent leavings   its heft   its inert and marigold
entangles

no longer damaged   the world

but   i n t a c t   i m m a c u l a t e

as   storm   light—

That was during my 56th year

to blacked-out, shiny heaven. Not

---

that I've been counting.

*

Reader, take note: when my myopic eyes were staring into the evil plastic door of the cell, at no point did it occur to me that it was time to quit drinking. On my own, that is. Amy agreed to stay with me if I got my habit under control, which I have, though she suffered a subdued anxiety attack when she attended a Remembrance Day ceremony the next month and saw RCMP officers.

Several memories linger for her: cops in our living room, tasers at hand; their inquiries about the lock she has on her bedroom door. Something else that remains: the difficulty she has when using the kitchen knives for cooking after seeing them jutting from my coat.

Over dinner that Sunday evening, I could barely eat a single piece of chicken. As we ate dinner, Jakob innocent of what had happened, I was quite aware of the plant behind me on the window sill. It had purple, oddly shaped petals, and she'd bought it for me that Sunday afternoon as a symbol of commitment. Since then it's been moved to a new place, but I check on it each Sunday to see whether it needs water, and to remember why it's in the house.

INTERLUDE: A SLOW-PACED, THOUGH GILDED, HYSTERIA

Clinical depression torpedoed my twenties, thirties, and early forties, though now that it's mostly retreated, anxiety has been quite pleased to take its place.[28] When it was very bad, depression sabotaged my memory: visiting extended family, I'd blank on my nieces' names or start saying something at the dinner table and then panic as I neared ending a sentence because I couldn't remember how it began. And all the while, I've learned that spiritual cowardice goes well with consistent drinking, and mixing the two works like this: you're kept safe, jubilantly solipsistic, spinning on the proverbial merry-go-round so pleasantly that nothing much can get

---

28   Depression is always lurking on the periphery, however, making its presence known through verbal tics: yesterday, for instance, when Amy was discussing Jakob's upcoming birthday party with him, the disease stabbed me, changing what she said. The word Amy used was "party," though I heard the word "funeral" slide on top of hers. The form this essay embodies—a kind of contemporary anatomy—possibly results from my residual depression. In *Black Sun: Depression and Melancholia*, one of the most accurate studies of depression I've read, Julia Kristeva notes: "Naming suffering, exalting it, dissecting it into its smallest components—this is doubtless a way to curb mourning" (97). In other words, the desire for greater and greater exactitude, which corresponds to the desire for more extensive and intricate elaboration as one writes, is feasibly a self-defensive strategy for keeping full-blown depression from arriving and making itself at home.

its hooks in, but the price seems to be more anxiety, not less of it, hard as these things are to quantify. You don't need to be an alcoholic to rely on how well a drink can defeat boredom, enliven indolence, make writing feel less like work, and ensure that you don't feel too deeply. No, that's not precise. You can have powerful emotions, and even allow yourself some vulnerability, but there's always a kind of slow-paced, though gilded, hysteria to each emotion, regardless of whether it's rage, spite, or serenity. There's an insulation to experience even if it's rampant with pleasure, as when one Sunday, when Lynn and I were students, just married, we drank wine, then listened to new cassette tapes—we were discovering classical music—and I convinced her to go for a walk though there was a storm, and I surprised her by gently pulling her down on the grass, lifting her top in the dark rain near the pond at York University, kissing her and then imitating a cockatiel: all of this to gratify the future by securing a memory that would keep. I was simultaneously sincere and acting something out, and I've no idea whether this memory has persisted for her. There's even an insulation to experience that you can't eradicate when you're sitting in a bathtub with one of the case cutters you've kept from the grocery store and are discovering cutting for the first time.

*

But the truth of excess, its value, is hard to discern because it dilates and shape-shifts: during one Sunday afternoon that was ablaze with chilled vodka, I sat in a room clogged with cigarette smoke, listened to Marilyn Manson and Kraftwerk repeatedly while staring into a blizzard and writing a poem about summer on a recently purchased TV dinner table I used for a desk (though back then I didn't own a TV). Most of the poem was written in one sitting on this scored wooden rectangle, onto which I'd taped a postcard of Munch's *Ashes* I'd bought in Oslo's Munch museum the previous August. Somehow the stained and slightly warped postcard survived it all, and is now just to my left considerably more than a decade later, propped up against the zebra-striped lamp that once lit the one-room apartment suite I secured after leaving Lynn and our kids. The poem was awarded first place in a contest by a journal that keeps rejecting my recent work, and it isn't as though the Muse favours inebriation over sobriety—both will either serve or not—but I do think every poem has within it a very specific genesis that only a precisely configured constellation of mood, luck, and circumstance can ultimately bring out.

*

I don't know how widespread regret is, but I'm curious to examine the various forms it can take, to see what it really holds. Let me get at this by listening to someone else: Jakob once told me that he and his friends in their imaginary town have a fire in which they roast souls and what this burning does, according to him, is take away what these souls "were good at." How could he know such a thing is possible?

The poems one does or doesn't write; the ones that never could be written.

Eli Mandel once confided to me that, after he'd completed a poem, he never knew if he would ever be a poet again. This made no sense to me: I was twenty-two, had just bought him a glass of his favourite Campari, had been trying to read some of the many books he'd spoken about, and I thought, then, that writing poetry meant hard work, sure, but that for someone like Eli, being a poet was a complex yet basic vocation, something continuous, something that he simply did—brilliantly. And I wanted to be like him. When I made these objections, his face took on an expression that meant he was going to offer something delightfully gnomic. "Do you know what W.H. Auden once said? He said that when a poet dies, God will greet him by reciting by heart all the poems the poet failed to write. By heart."

It's been over thirty years since we had that conversation, and Eli's gone, but I've thought of those two moments often—when Eli stood beside me in the Absinthe bar at Winter's College at York after a class, and also the celestial moment—and I've wondered whether God is brutal or speaks with compassionate regret when he takes you in hand. But I've discovered by chance that Eli didn't cite Auden accurately. He left something out, and what he missed was crucial. I'd always assumed it had been something Auden might have said in an interview, but his remarks are in a poem: I wasn't thinking either of Auden or Eli when I recently read a Hannah Arendt essay, and was taken aback to see that she'd selected a portion of Auden's poem "The Cave of Making" for an epigraph. I'd never seen these words in print, and Eli was right that God addresses the poet directly. But here's the rub: while God's private attitude toward these unwritten poems isn't clear, the poet, upon hearing God's recitation on Judgment Day, will, significantly, be reduced "to tears of shame" upon hearing the various poems

                          you would
               have written, had
                    your life been good.

The disparity between God reciting a poet's unwritten poems—we all
have those for various reasons—versus those he, she, or they might have
written if one's life had been good, feels like being stung awake by a
wasp you've rolled upon in the night. The point isn't that moral people
write better or more poems than immoral ones. Nor is it that ethical
sloth stands in the way of new poems, though that's closer, I think, to
what Auden means. Each writer must take this admonition personally,
because, when honest, I suspect that he or she already senses the sort of
life that would be necessary to work towards this obligatory (and perhaps
unreachable) integrity. I know how my continual evasion has gradually
created a life of inanity that I'm fairly certain could have been avoided,
at least partially. But how can someone accomplish the life Auden intimates, so as to create those poems that risk going astray? How many of
these poems are there, and how will they sound when you hear them
spoken? How can one live so as not to have to experience the humilia-
tion and shame of hearing for the first time those refulgent poems with
which God is so familiar?

   Now that I'm learning something about failure, I'm getting closer to
becoming the person Eli was actually speaking to while I was drinking
beer alongside him. If I could join him again, I'd ask him this question,
the one I fear the most: what, Eli, what do you do if the talent that's
needed to write those poems that God may one day recite by heart, what
happens if that talent got destroyed before it could ever be used? And
then a further question: how can one gain the wisdom to avoid despair
and develop the gratitude for what one actually has? But these questions
are unanswerable. And the last time I saw Eli it was after he'd suffered
the first of several strokes, and he was being pushed in a wheelchair by
his wife into the Yorkdale Cinemas in Toronto to watch *A Fish Called
Wanda*. Lynn and I, who'd met in one of Eli's classes, had gone to the
movie to escape the sweltering heat and humidity in our cockroach-in-
fested apartment in Toronto. He looked our way, but offered no sign of
recognition.

THE GUARD IN THE MUSEUM

Sunday, October 23, 2016

A week ago Cell 23… and this morning a Starbucks coffee and a Sunday *New York Times* that I'm reading in New York, not something I've ever done. Back home, the paper doesn't arrive until Wednesday. During my time in Cell 23, I thought I should cancel my long-awaited trip to NYC, uncertain what I'd do left to myself in a city of excess. But here I am. The mirror in the cramped room in the Belnord Hotel contains an unshaven man, wearing the same shirt worn last Sunday, not for penance, but as a reminder: sober for a week. Somehow abstinent in the city where Lynn and I went on our honeymoon in 1985. Somehow bruised, restrained in the same city in which—there for the first time only a few years before I married Lynn, I sat for some God-given hours amidst garbage on 42nd Street with Kelly, my oldest friend. Back then, 42nd was ablaze with sex shows, whatever drugs took your interest, in-your-face pimps, and vanishing hotels. Every so often my cigarette lighter flicked out a tiny blue flame like a gagging snake. Both of us drank out of bottles in paper bags, watching what could have been spooled out of a Lou Reed album; but we were two small-town boys from southern Ontario, sitting there amidst the cardboard boxes and garbage bags, the two of us slippery as sun on bricks, psycho-surfing inside the joy of being young and recognized by no one.

And now, some three decades later, when I look inside, I see what anyone would expect. Anguish, guilt, a very small bit of pride, gratitude to Amy, curiosity about this new sensation of booze leaving my system, panic about having to get my life right, shame. A small bit of patience, something of which Don Gately, David Foster Wallace's recovering drug addict, would approve. Holding it steady. I've brought *Infinite Jest* with me, deciding that now is the time finally to read it. And I learn quickly enough that nobody gets those two predators—addiction and depression—as right as Wallace does. My flight to New York last Thursday was delayed over eight hours, which meant reading the novel one chapter after another, getting up sporadically from the waiting lounge and shouldering my carry-on luggage to get one green tea after another, then finding a new place to sit, all within that surrounding mood that only airports offer: a loop of sullen, wired anticipation. If insomnia could be spatialized, it would be an airport lounge filled with people sloped on that style of chairs so favoured by those who design hubs of transportation: chairs linked together in small groups. An incongruous play structure has been placed near a window; the small slide and beaded wires give the appearance of worn-down equipment used for experimental studies in psychology. This place is what waiting entails for the modern version of the mostly-middle-class human creature. Everything—from cranky or listless children to the TVs overhead and even the nearby and astringent future buckling with disdain—everything is eavesdropping on itself. The minutes pass. Existence in airports is unconvincing.

The 4:00 a.m. cab ride from Newark to West 89th cost over $100, despite how fast we were moving through the unexpectedly empty freeways to the city. The first time I'd gone from New Jersey to Manhattan was during the early '80s. I'd taken a bus, was twenty-two, and was utterly bereft for the first time in my life because of my breakup with my common-law partner Cindy. Laurie Anderson hadn't met Lou Reed. Jean Basquiat was still painting. Back then, Donald Trump was only what he's always been. And of course the people inside the Twin Towers were simply spending another day at work that day.

*

As I leave the hotel room, about to go to the Whitney, but mostly to wander for much of the day, I lock the door and then check it, and with a slight push, it springs open. Instant anxiety: alive and rushing toward me down the hallway. *Anyone can break in.* I wait for the hotel handyman to come and fix it. When he does, he works quietly, using a metal file to repair what separates the inside from the outside. He's

Hispanic, like all of the other hotel employees I see. I give him a dollar, which surprises him, and as he gives me a slight bow, I wonder what his apartment looks like when he returns after a day's work. I've always been drawn to Geoff Dyer's quip that New York is home for people who have never felt at home.

While walking down Amsterdam Avenue yesterday morning, I recognized a bar from a trip I'd made in 2009. It was irresistible back then. I'd gone there very late one night, drunk, and left, a little bit more blurred. Bar's name? Dead Poet, and I remember choosing a beer called Delirium Tremens. Fortunately, not something I've known.

Stopping to look at the Dakota Apartments, I hear one young man telling his two friends about Mark Chapman and *Catcher in the Rye*; none of them was alive on December 8, 1980. A Monday.

*

New York is a place where predicaments disappear not quite forever. A man who is used to the street answers my gaze by asking whether my Tragically Hip T-shirt means I'm from Canada. Now that he has me, he tells me to listen, just listen to the river underneath the subway: I'm telling you, sir: you can hear sacred ॐ, he says. And will you buy this poem from me? He shows several sheets of paper on which many copies of his haiku are printed. Its title is *Chiri Naki*, he says, which means "without dust." He reads the poem, making a half circle with his arm, and then tears one off from the rest and shows it to me:

> Each child from here
> to Spain opens a can of
> soda all at once!

Why Spain? It's on the ocean, he says, and it's got one syllable. Five dollars works. And then he wants to shake my hand. A woman walks south with many flying fish tattooed up her left leg from ankle to crotch. A man in a motorized wheelchair is close behind her, a breathing tube in his nostrils tethered to his oxygen tank. Seeing him, the baseball cap on his head, his sunken interiority, I think that the only substantial thing I've done in the days between Cell 23 and today was talk on the phone with Maurice Elliott.

Maurice was a colleague of Eli Mandel's at York University, and I took some English courses from him. But when we spoke last week, he'd been incapacitated by Multiple Systems Atrophy (MSA) for several years and was living in a care facility outside Toronto because his wife had recently become unable to look after him. A mutual friend had alerted me to his illness two years before; if he hadn't developed this rare neurological disease I wouldn't have re-established contact, not having seen him since the mid-1980s. Until his wife got him a phone headset, during some of our conversations, his skull would be involuntarily pulled towards his chest—a condition called disproportionate antecollis—and I could only hear him intermittently then, sometimes with ten minutes or so going by this way. He grieved that no one—not his children, nor any library or bookseller—was interested in the thousands of volumes he'd accumulated over a lifetime. When I called him last week at the care home, his wife answered, gratitude in her voice, saying that she would leave then because Maurice would be called for supper after our conversation was over. "I hate it here," he told me. When he heard about my NYC trip, he said, apologetically, "I hope that you don't mind if I tell you I'm envious." On only one other occasion have I been in the proximity of such living hurt.

*

I once was alone in a room with a poet who was in his first month of being totally cut off from the world because of ALS. Over a few years he'd been slowly reduced to using his left eyelid to blink as a form of communication, but that final ability had been shut down. When I went to his room I greeted him in his enormous wheelchair, stayed for I don't know how long, read him some of his poetry, tried to find something to say that couldn't possibly have any painful associations. There was a kind of immobile watching somewhere behind his eyes, perhaps imagined on my part, and it was only this sign of presence that suggested any kind of movement. Whether this man recognized me, wanted my company, or would have preferred that I find and play his favourite music from the pile of CDs by the window... all of these things remained entirely incarcerated behind his eyes, they seeming to grow larger as I glanced at them to discover what he may have wanted to say. How to place words before the abyss when one is healthy? How to speak to someone in that state from within the safe receptacle of one's own mind inside a body that works? This poet had himself written a poem to a fellow poet who had been "lopsided" by a stroke and unable to communicate.

A generous man who loved and enthused about Lamb and Hazlitt, Maurice hosted a poetry series at York and invited me to a private supper with Seamus Heaney after Heaney had read from his newly published *Station Island*, and then he sat me to Heaney's right at the table. Rarely have I felt so undeservedly lucky and helplessly stupid as when Heaney went out of his way to express interest in this ridiculously unread young man who could only go on about how he found the title poem's imagined conversation with Joyce to contain great advice and to be very moving.

As time will obliterate the conversations I shared with Maurice, what will likely (and maybe unfortunately) remain intact within me will be the anguish in his husky voice as we said goodbye during one of our calls, and he cried out to me "Keep reading!" This was an expression driven from his innermost self, of which I knew very little, though I did recognize his need to retain his value as my mentor as much as he was simultaneously crying out to reading itself, one of the most sustaining foundations his life had made for him. In this chat, of his many recommendations, he told me I should read some Annie Dillard and then Oswald Spengler. It took about thirty years from when he'd taught me to hear Wordsworth for his illness to begin, and I feel like puking whenever I think of him learning "solitude, pain of heart, distress" from within his own unsettled brain's body. As a student, I loved when profs recommended books, and I can recall that he recommended we read Barbellion's *Diary of a Disappointed Man*, an early-twentieth-century diary detailing the author's defiant collapse as he suffered and then died from MS. I found a remaindered copy, though I have never read it… what is terribly disturbing is that I can only assume that Maurice either reread the book or thought about it as he became steadily more incapacitated.

*

Because it's Sunday, the Grand Bazaar flea market is open. I'd forgotten that I'd gone there in 2009. I buy Amy a jet Victorian brooch, two antique marbles, and a plastic monkey. As I'm shopping, I realize that, had I taken a different direction, I would have missed the market and thereby not accidentally revived the memory from my previous visit. Where has this latent memory resided in the intervening years, something that I'd forgotten I knew? Our sense of what has brought us to the present is so infinitesimal; it's as if we only meet ourselves when we stumble upon who we are by blunt contingency. Seen this way, we're doomed to be careless, even ludicrous creatures. Caricatures, almost, of what we really are. That we are oblivious to much of who we are impoverishes our lives, but it is obviously unavoidable, not simply because memory is faulty, but because the present cascades with such authority (to mix metaphors) that it diverts almost all of our attention to the moment that's passing through us. For me, almost all the time, news of my forgetfulness is merely information—I'm too busy living to take account of psychological metaphysics. I suspect most others are similarly negligent. But our uncertain grasp of ourselves undermines everything: our sense of ongoing reality, our love for others. Item: a person discovers that a partner doesn't recall a single detail from a shared experience that the former cherishes. Nada, not one. What can love mean, then, when we can't coincide with the person whom we love? There must be a deep fissure of loneliness within each person's experience of the present. Every moment must contain an infinite number of temporalities, but again, we don't notice this complexity, except perhaps when we encounter extreme instances of people being locked inside their own lives. When I spoke to Maurice on the phone I invariably found this prospect to be horrifying. During the part of his life when he suffered MSA, the present must have bored down into him with a terrible, debilitating violence… and yet, to have heard him read Dickens aloud or recite by memory various stanzas from Wordsworth was to have been welcomed into a wonderful moment that happened in several modes of time simultaneously. Even today, I can hear him reciting "Lines Composed a Few Miles above Tintern Abbey" during those moments when the class was occurring in 1983, but these words—words with which he was thoroughly familiar and had repeated so many times—had arisen in the eighteenth century.

It turns out that on that Sunday I was in New York, October 23, he had less than two months left to live, and when his widow emailed me to ask if I wanted any of Maurice's books, I asked her if I could have one of his copies of Wordsworth. She gave me his edition that was published in 1889. I'll never know precisely what he felt during his anguished admonition that I should keep reading, but he was trying to connect with something bigger than offering encouragement to the middle-aged man his former student had become. He was waving from the abyss.

116

Working in a grocery store provided the savings to give me a backpacking trip to Europe when I was a teenager, and this trip introduced me to modern art. If it pains me that I can never be more than a compulsive dilettante about painting, my ignorance when I went to New York for the first time in 1982 was marvelous because it meant that almost all of the artists who were exhibited in the museums were new to me. I still have postcards I bought from that trip showing work by de Chirico, Frida Kahlo, and Paul Klee. I've moved more than twenty times since that trip, and these cards have decorated as many walls. Paul Klee's *The Red Balloon* is taped to the window frame in front of my writing space. Almost forty years old, age has given the postcard a nice wabi sabi wear to it… Klee might like how it appears today.

Leaving the Grand Bazaar, I went through Strawberry Fields in Central Park, heading toward the Whitney, but I didn't know it had moved downtown since I'd been there last. It was now the Met Breuer. Two exhibits were showing: a Diane Arbus retrospective and the Bergruen Paul Klee collection. Many of the Arbus pictures I'd never seen, especially early images of children about to cross a curb into an empty street, one of a girl carrying schoolbooks, the other a boy turning toward Arbus. Different from the girl heading home, this boy is aware of Arbus taking his picture. His face and right hand, his socks, glow against his dark clothes, the slightly sodden street, and within his eyes it's as though his entire life, the one that will ensue after his encounter with the woman with her camera, is present, looking at the viewer—year upon year, from his maturity to that unexpected childhood moment in 1957. And now all of him visible and invisible to us. I always do the arithmetic of people's lives—Arbus 1923 to 1971 = 48 years—and I hoped that, whoever that boy was, he was still alive on that October day in 2016.

I hope that he is alive even more in today's now. Against these thoughts, formed while thinking of that trip in 2016, I recall that there was also a ghastly image I've never seen reproduced of an old woman dying; she would have been born in the nineteenth century, Arbus's own life framed entirely by the twentieth.

Going upstairs to the Klee exhibit, I wanted *The Red Balloon* to be there. It wasn't, of course, belonging to the Guggenheim, not to the collection on show. But I searched anyway. Before going to this exhibit, I knew almost nothing of Klee's life. The discovery that systemic scleroderma had struck him at age fifty-seven, killing him four years later, greatly unnerved me. This new knowledge gave a dimension to his work (especially that created near the end of his life) that I hadn't anticipated when I opened the door from the stairwell to view the exhibit. I was diagnosed with morphea, a type of scleroderma, in my early forties, though it's now in remission. It's an autoimmune disease: what happens is that the body starts eating itself. When my two kids with Lynn were very young, I used to bathe with them, and one evening my son Jesse pointed to a small lesion on my right leg, wanting to know what it was. He was sitting between my legs facing the same direction as I was. I had no idea where the grey-red mottled mark had come from, but after going through several doctors, I learned the diagnosis. The morphea spread down one leg and then did the same with the other. Scleroderma is rare: I was told that only 70 people in all of Saskatchewan have it… and today my right quadriceps muscle looks as though a small shark once attacked it. I was assured by a rheumatologist that my condition almost never developed into the far more dangerous systemic form of the disease. The pain lasted for about two years and was exhausting. I took to sleeping for much of the day when I wasn't working.

> It penetrates so deeply and so gently into me. I feel it and it gives me confidence in myself without effort. Color has got me. I don't have to pursue it. It will possess me always, I know it. That is the meaning of this happy hour, color and I are one. I am a painter.
> —Paul Klee, diary, April 16, 1914

All of this was yet to come when I came upon *The Red Balloon* in 1982. The medical health of someone looking at a painting is obviously irrelevant to the work itself, but learning of Klee's scleroderma made me look more closely at the other people going through the exhibit. Until then, I'd thought Munch was the painter who most opened his canvases to a specific brand of human frailty shared by him and his viewers, but I began to see how Klee's hermetic works extended beyond the canvas, nearing upon whomever got close. I've got nothing original to say about Klee's beguiling and cryptic personal iconography, beguiling partially because we have no access to Klee's feelings as he created one portal after another, each drawing or painting a place where his inner landscape merged with the other invisible one perhaps only he could sense. What we do have is that his warmer works seem to offer the viewer what he or she needs the most—for me that day, a second chance—and for the forbidding ones like *A Girl in Mourning*, a kind of stupefied fear from which one recoils. Seeing a person leaning on a cane in front of one of Klee's paintings of birds, I thought of the envy Maurice had for me when he learned of this trip. Still thinking of him, I walked through Central Park, rejuvenated by what I'd seen in the gallery, and jubilant as well to wander beneath the sky that was a subdued just-about-to-rain. I wished he could have been eavesdropping with me when I heard the following exchange:

1st man: these robots, they think they are us

2nd man: we don't know *squat*… Ed Harris is a billionaire… he's the man to watch

1st man: there's a deeper level to the game

*

Inside joy, three things to retain:

… everything I value most is on loan, no more mine or of my making than the generative, sustaining light of the sun… I've been made aware that the world I dwell in has been furnished almost entirely by others, only rarely with my particular well-being in mind but to my lasting benefit all the same…
—Edwin Dobb, "Nothing but Gifts: Finding a Home in a World Gone Awry"

Alongside *The Red Balloon*:

Even the blossoming tree lies the moment its bloom is seen without the shadow of terror; even the innocent "How lovely!" becomes an excuse for an existence outrageously unlovely, and there is no beauty or consolation except in the gaze falling on horror, withstanding it, and in unalleviated consciousness of negativity holding fast to the possibility of what is better.
—Theodor Adorno, *Minima Moralia: Reflections on a Damaged Life*

Well, that's my lecture… And now we're gonna travel.
—Agnes Martin, *Paintings, Writings, Remembrances*

But how can one do this, *withstand* something like the life of Fakhra Yunnus, a woman facially disfigured by an acid attack, *travel* with her, or even write about her today?

*

Having bought Amy the Victorian brooch at the flea market, I wanted to get something for Jakob; thinking that the Museum of Natural History would likely have a dinosaur to add to his collection, I went inside and to my surprise saw that the gift shop wasn't open to passersby as most museum shops are. Only ticket holders could go past the lobby and enter the store.

From my 2016 diary:
But what I'm really interested in regarding faces is *The Denial of Saint Peter* by Caravaggio, in the Met. That look someone has when lying and knowing one is lying and splitting the mind between lying and recognizing the lie. (Like Karl Ove Knausgaard's mother-in-law lying about drinking while babysitting his kids.) What I want to see is the moment not of emergent sensation, but of putting a question to one's self, a moment that breaks the temporal flow of associative thought. I'm intrigued because it forces us, in either a major way (Saint Peter) or minor one (guard at the Natural History Museum deciding whether to give me permission to break the rules and go downstairs to buy a toy for Jakob) to be in a situation where the self must question itself, and in doing so, a temporary judgment is incurred.

Light the Inscrutable Shade of Neon Nail Polish

What can I know? What ought I to do? What may I expect?
—Immanuel Kant, 1787

A moment untracked by Big Tech: the guard at the Museum of Natural History in New York pondering my request to go downstairs to the gift shop without paying the admission fee because I want to buy a present for my son back in Canada, but I promise that I won't stay to see the exhibits? Instantly, his entire face registers this change in routine. Behind eyes that stop watching the crowd—their gaze receding and then coming to a rest somewhere invisible to me—his mind unexpectedly becomes alert to ethics and choice. Staying employed. Remarkable to observe the facial expression of a mind privately questioning itself. Looking for clues. After a few seconds: *Go over there and ask the other guard at the main entrance.*

Moving amongst school children, beneath the skeleton of a plant-eating dinosaur, and past lineups of people using credit cards with microchips to pay for tickets, I repeated my question to the other guard. His gleaming shoes rocked slightly on the marble floor. Pondering the matter for five or six breaths, with an identical, utterly quiet countenance—how could their facial gestures so mirror each other?—then a stern nod to me and next... a different kind of nod to the guard I first approached, who was watching from across the lobby. What was the history embedded in the look passed between them?

> —all machine-learning algorithms are black boxes, but the human
> brain is a black box, says Richard Burk, a professor of criminology
> and stats, a man who favours blue jeans, a wedding band, and gazes
> downward at the camera—

Down two flights of stairs, I found some surprisingly impressive velociraptor stuffies for my son, a necklace with an ant inside an amber pendant, and an intensely beautiful statue of Osiris, the length of an index finger and much heavier than I thought it should be. The god's eyes the inscrutable shade of neon nail polish.   Outside, a continuously incomplete sky, alive
with doubt and loopable white noise, the late afternoon as malleable as heated lead: there's nothing inevitable about this rainy place, except those wet petals near the shrubs, except these cement curbs splashing and splashed by cars and cars and a steady blur of passersby: a duration of people has always slowly vanished as they keep going by...

and inside is   outside is
algorithms always following you:
but where are you
where *are* you
traced

→ from last night's movie-mind-caress → to this morning's latté →
to your favourite methadone clinic in the mall... granular surveillance

traffics in   makes a sweep through   What
can I know?   What
ought I to do?   What
may I expect?

grain… by… grain… by grain… and who… ?
knows? —who decides who knows? *Who decides
who decides who knows?*—
—Shoshana Zuboff, author of *Surveillance Capitalism*
in 2020 inside
the struggle
to preserve
the center of
our undirected
anxiety

BASKETBALL, JOHN LENNON, AND A HELICOPTER

Sunday, January 26, 2020

Upon returning from Edmonton that afternoon, I checked the news to learn that Kobe Bryant had just died in a helicopter crash with his daughter Gianna (1978–2020; 2007–2020). I immediately emailed my son Jesse to express condolences because I knew how much he admired Kobe as a basketball player. I'd been in Edmonton over the weekend to watch Jesse play university ball for the MacEwan Griffins. While there, I sat with Lynn in the bleachers and watched him play well, though his team lost every game that season. Shortly after I sent the email, Jess replied, thanking me for reaching out and telling me that Bryant had been his hero while growing up and that life was cruel to kill him and his daughter. He was genuinely shaken up, and would be so for a few weeks.

Contingency: after our divorce, Lynn married a man who is a fervent basketball fan, encouraging Jesse to start playing around age 6 and going so far as to have an extension built on his house so it could include a small gym for his own son and Jesse to use. Had Lynn and I stayed together, it's unlikely that basketball would have become the focus of Jesse's life, given that she and I had little interest in sports.

Choice: I too had had a hero when I was a teenager. Born too late to be a baby boomer (to me, in order to belong to this generation, you had to be old enough to do drugs and have sex at Woodstock, but I was only 9 that summer), I had an ardent passion for the '60s and became a hippy wannabe. John Lennon's music and politics were behind my joining Amnesty International, but I deliberately idealized him over the other Beatles because I knew that my conventional southern-Ontario mother had no use for him and in fact despised people like him. Later, it was his capacity to write clean, almost minimalist songs when he wasn't embodying a watered-down surrealism that made me a fan. I wore white when I could, and I wept when he died on December 8, 1980, though Cindy would later mock me for being maudlin. I play Lennon music each anniversary, including the December 8 that held Maurice's death in 2016.

My trip to Edmonton was also made to spend time with Andy, drinking tea and learning about their journalism program. I also hoped that my visit would partially compensate for how few games of Jesse's I attended when he lived in Regina. My attendance was irregular; Lynn, on the other hand, took in every game she could and helped him record a video CV that impressed university team coaches. The weekend did cement the two of us more, I think, and I have a Polaroid photo of an aging man with his arm around his taller son in his uniform on the court after the final game. Who is he, my eldest son? A stronger, calmer, and more generous man than his father. To watch anyone score a 3-point basket with perfect grace is a kind of beauty that is similar to coming across a grebe or merganser unexpectedly. The beauty is so pure. When it's your own son, it feels as though every cell in your body is bright with excitement.

It was on this visit that I encouraged Andy to submit a creative nonfiction essay to a journal, and the publication is now in the stack of books on my writing desk. Called "Chlorine Head," the essay entails their own difficulties with depression, alternating success/failure with meds, and "queer joy." I shared it with Philip, my historian friend, and he thought Andy's writing resembles mine, except that theirs is more blistering. Despite its clear-eyed misery, the essay is a 3-point basket in prose.

It seemed to me when my kids were quite young that Andy resembled me and Jesse resembled Lynn as far as personality goes, but as always, things are more complicated. (In 2016 when I returned from New York, I brought home Lakers paraphernalia for Jesse and for Andy, a body-length scarf emblazoned with skulls.)

*

When I first started noticing time in late childhood, I thought that the lives my family and I were living weren't yet what would become our actual lives; they were pretend—not quite a rehearsal; more a kind of ongoing dawdling before the signal would be given (though where the signal would come from I didn't know) and then: real life would begin. It took me years to recognize that this foray into metaphysics was partially made possible by the protected childhood my professional parents offered my sisters and me—father a teacher, mother a nurse (at that point comfortably married). Part of me felt like a sightseer visiting our lives. And then one day in 2003 when I had my own children, I was astounded to hear my son Jesse respond similarly. Perhaps part of what it means to be a child is that something adults casually classify as "dream-like" is embedded within the urgency of a child's immediate experience, so that maybe many children find their lives to be an intensely felt mirage that also seems naturally cyclical. Watching my children chance upon time as a force that's somehow part of us but separate as well wasn't something I could have anticipated. I hoped to get closer to the inherent complexity of what was happening by writing about it.

This Afternoon

we're in the park throwing pennies
into the magic fountain, magic because at Christmas
the water somehow turns into falling loops
and stranded archways—a precise havoc
of happy streaming electric lights.

The stone fish who live here all year round

like the summer best, we
decide. And then one of the new
fathers goes running by, pushing someone in a slick
three wheeler, a drag racer burning up the path, and my son (four
this month) wants to know: when I become a baby again
can you get me
one of those?

His sister jumps in, tells him he'll never be a baby
again, but O God, neither of them
sees the distance taking shape
in her news. Until then

I'd thought he'd taken mostly
after his mother / our daughter,
me. Once

she stalled me when out of a chaos
of letters   she formed her first

correctly spelled word: *cat.* And
a bubble cracked inside showing me

showing my mother a mad map of paper
with the word *cat* on it, just like
hers, wrestled from a child's magic
marker cabbala / a fluke
                              no doubt. But today
I'm looking out of my old bedroom window, it's another
afternoon, a Sunday in August I think. I'm ten again

for the first time, and there's some guys I've never
liked playing street hockey, and I've been waiting

for the moment when it would
all begin again, when this watery

life would finally start for real—so that ten
years later I'd find myself exactly ten
again looking out my bedroom
window / and finding Mom
in the far away

kitchen down the hall. She's canning and I sit
cross-legged on the floor, look up (the
Portuguese rooster's still there) and ask her if life happens
twice—would we be going to the beach again someday
the same way we'd done last weekend? When does
everything come back? But I didn't really
need to ask, I already half / knew
what she'd say.
                    And so tonight,
my heart is travelling

in flame—what made him, what made
my son, see the perfect ride and want
to make sure that when he became
a baby again that it
would be his?

Perhaps everyone feels the sift
of metaphysics, except
my daughter already knows
it's not like that. This

then is my prayer—may neither
of them choose to see how
appealing it is to take a fingernail
and slice open the present
to find what's missing in the long rooms
there.   Let them find instead

their mother's voice
listening, always listening, the way
she listens inside them.

    If Jesse and I expected we'd eventually return to another life in this world again, but with our subsequent existences improving on the first, I wonder how much this desire persists into adulthood, taking on different guises. And it's with this longing that words come into play. But I don't think our lives are long enough to grasp what occurs within us as we encounter language. Perhaps reading and writing engage an innate need for repetition, and then, finally, to get things right, though one of my greatest concerns is that, because of aging and substance abuse, I don't know if my brain still has the elasticity required to write poems like the one above anymore.

*

How many children of my generation internalized the Cold War? I can recall watching *Fail-Safe*, a movie about nuclear apocalypse, with my dad when I was very young. The movie gave me a recurrent nightmare that I can still feel. It goes like this: I'm alone in a small room that somehow is and isn't my bedroom. Against the wall I'm facing, there's this series of numbers going from left to right, up near the ceiling: one through ten. A voice tells me that I have to choose a number and if I choose incorrectly, the bombs begin. So there's a 10% chance of stopping everyone's death. Of course I choose wrongly, and the dream ends with bombs going off outside my window down the street. If I'd chosen the right number, we'd all be alive. (Recalling this dream, now, I can barely see the screen because of tears.) I don't know if anyone has tried to measure the subconscious lives of children in different historical periods, but I can say that, as a professor, I've discovered very happily that none of my students have had these nightmares as children.[29] Looking back, I suspect that these two reactions to childhood—the sense that the present isn't quite real and the fear of inevitable apocalypse—has gone far to form the basis of my psyche's interaction with the world.

The Nights the Child Dreams of Numbers

A child wakes inside someone sitting
on a small bed in a different room

the door is hiding   it's not where doors
used to be and up near the ceiling some

numbers appear   one through ten
just as the alphabet does at school

it's dark and each number glows in its own
circle   unforgiving as the clock above

the teacher's desk and a man's voice wearing
a Sunday-sounding suit and tie   he keeps saying

to choose a number   choose   but the child knows
the wrong word will make the bombs

---

29   Last week Jakob dreamed of using a taser on a tiger. He interpreted this dream to mean that his personal use of electricity is causing global warming.

begin   but guess right: 1 out of 10
and then everyone in the world won't

have to die   but the child's alone and no
one else can hear   no help   it's like

a secret kept from everyone
outside
of the room and all the families

stay sleeping safe inside   the man's voice
is watching from somewhere   breathing

far away but grownup and clear *choose
now* the man insists and the child sitting

on the bed says a number that's never
recalled as the dream always

obliterates its own ending   and this is
what is

this now
that's becoming
unreachable—

*

Shortly after Bryant and his daughter's accidental death, *The New York Times Sunday Magazine* featured an article on Anselm Kiefer written by Karl Ove Knausgaard. Both artists appeal to me greatly, especially Kiefer, whose multi-generic work transforms the elegiac in its mourning of the twentieth century.

In the interview, published in February 2020, Kiefer advises Knausgaard to buy a helicopter as they spend a few days going through his various projects in rooms as large as airplane hangars; Kiefer's studio is a world within a world, offers the Norwegian. Again, I envy artists who can create images that then are also composed of various material substances, rather than just words. Simon Schama perfectly describes Kiefer's piece *Hosanna*—comprised of graphite and sand—that it is "simultaneously biological and cosmological… [and] this is as good, I think, as art ever gets: mystery and matter delivered in a rush of poetic illumination." And Schama's definition of art is as close to a concise definition of art's manner as I've ever encountered.

When I read of Keifer's favoured mode of transportation, I couldn't help but recall the helicopter that crashed in California on January 26. I won't ask anything more than this roughly hewn question: of what does our civilization consist in its encounter with global warming, COVID rapidly moving across the world, and all the while, those who belong to the wealthy 1% prefer to travel by helicopter?

> Change is caused by lazy, greedy, frightened people looking for easier, more profitable, and safer ways to do things…. But that is not the end of the story… humans… invented style.
> —Ian Morris, *Why the West Rules—For Now: The Patterns of History, and What They Reveal About the Future*

CONTOURS

Is it possible that we thought we had to retrieve what happened
before we were born?
— Rainer Maria Rilke, *The Notebooks of Malte Laurids Brigge*

CONTOURS: IN SEARCH OF ETTY HILLESUM

(A Lyric Documentary)

Foreword

Exuberant, yet aware of the monstrous confusions of her time, Etty Hillesum was one of the Holocaust's most important diarists. Astutely perceptive of the psychologies of both victims and perpetrators, owing perhaps to her own depressive mood disorders, she wrote from within the chaos imposed by the Nazis, refused to go into hiding, and eventually died at Auschwitz.

If Hillesum couldn't envision what the camps meant from her vantage point of Amsterdam, neither can twenty-first-century readers (innocently) see her work on its own terms because we can't pass over why she died. This rift creates an insurmountable problem: as much as we might desire to approach her writing in a spirit similar to that with which she engaged her beloved Rilke, we necessarily become stalled because Auschwitz is a divide that can't be bridged. And yet to see her primarily as a Holocaust victim is to distort her life through a kind of blindness.

Thinking about Hillesum, however, means thinking about what was destroyed alongside her, and the forms this destruction took. To consider a place like Auschwitz requires us not only to begin paying attention to lives and events that proliferate beyond measure, but also to (self-consciously) work out new ways of sensing how much of that history has been irrevocably lost.

Here is a schedule listing a few train departures from Westerbork, the central Dutch location from where people were sent east:

Date	Year	Deportees	Destination
20 July	1943	2209	Sobibór
24 August	1943	1001	Auschwitz
31 August	1943	1004	Auschwitz
7 September	1943	987	Auschwitz

Four transports; each, as Hillesum noted, unique. But of these 5,201 people, 4,123 were gassed on arrival, and only one transport is generally known today, the one on which Hillesum and her parents were deported on September 7, 1943. To ponder Hillesum's life, then, entails imagining it within a mesh of circumstances that is almost entirely lost to view. What's at stake in this task?

Let me refer again to Ulrich Baer's *Spectral Evidence: The Photography of Trauma*, in which he contrasts the traditional "model of time-as-river" by setting it against its "counterpart... the Democritean conception of the world as occurring in bursts and explosions, as the rainfall of reality [which] privileges the moment rather than the story, the event rather than the unfolding, particularity rather than generality." Trying to encounter Hillesum from the perspective of the present, travelling to places she'd been (Amsterdam, Westerbork, Auschwitz), I began to perceive the problems of ascertaining the nature of simultaneity, of the "rainfall of reality" that surrounded her and through which she moved, its myriad people and occasions that coalesce and then dissipate. An incalculable immensity overtakes particular details, subsumes them, yet it is primarily from particulars and their connections that we have any sense of what happened.

When Eva Hoffman draws parallels between Hillesum's close friends (who urged her to save herself) and a "reader who comes to love Etty through her writing," she implicitly invites the question of how one might respond to the letters and diaries specifically through one's own writing. If it seems not only absurd but affected to address Hillesum directly, it is by no means clear what sort of addressee is suitable for such a project.

Leon Greenman, Etty Hillesum, Philip Mechanicus, Rudolf Werner Breslauer, Anne Frank

… were five people who lived during the Nazi occupation of Holland and left records of their experience. Each saw Westerbork, a transit camp in northern Holland through which 101,000 people passed, almost all Jews, primarily to Sobibór and Auschwitz-Birkenau.

Two of these people knew each other, Hillesum and Mechanicus, both of whom wrote about Westerbork, occasionally referring to the same event in their work. Mechanicus's diary begins on Friday, May 28, 1943. Unknown to them, Greenman and his family had already been deported to Birkenau, where his wife and child were murdered shortly after they waved to him from the truck that took them away. Hillesum and most of her family were deported on September 7, 1943. Her parents, Rebecca and Louis, were either dead or were gassed upon arrival at Birkenau; no one today knows what happened. Her brother Jaap was sent to Westerbork shortly after his family, but none of them were there when he stepped off the train from Amsterdam because they'd already been sent east; none of the family survived. Breslauer filmed Westerbork at the behest of the Kommandant, Albert Gemmeker; the most reproduced image from this movie is the seven-second clip showing a child looking out of a cattle car. It was long assumed that she was Jewish, and as such she became iconographic of Jewish children murdered in the Holocaust. It took until 2005 for a Dutch investigative journalist to discover that she was Sinti. Originally promised protection, Breslauer was likely killed upon arrival at Birkenau on October 24, 1944, two days before his family arrived from Terezín. Only his daughter, Ursula, survived. The Frank family was kept briefly in the punishment cell at Westerbork before being sent to Auschwitz. The transport upon which they travelled was the final one to leave Holland for that camp. Mechanicus was shot in Auschwitz on October 12, 1944. He'd been deported on March 8, 1944, and no one today knows anything of his life between those two dates. Kommandant Gemmeker spent six years in prison and lived until he was 75, dying in his hometown of Dusseldorf in 1982.

Transports from Westerbork frequently left on Tuesdays; often, those deported were informed as late as 3:00 a.m. to prepare their belongings and families for the morning's departure. Sometimes people whose names hadn't been announced the night before, and who thus thought they were safe for at least one more week, were seized without warning and placed on a train that hadn't yet filled its quota. A survivor of Westerbork whose 1962 interview is part of a continuous loop on a video screen at Washington's Holocaust Memorial Museum tells of how those Tuesdays at Westerbork keep returning to him every subsequent Tuesday.

Dinsdag. Dinsdag. Dinsdag.

Mechanicus noted a child's nightmare in his diary: her doll is being sent on a transport alone.

A 1/2 moon over Oświeçim

was just above and to the right of the *Arbeit Macht Frei* sign when I visited Auschwitz on a late Friday afternoon, having travelled by train from Warsaw early that morning. The moon wasn't my first impression upon entering the camp, certainly, but only two days before, I'd picked up Jakob (then a baby) as I did most nights back in Saskatchewan before I went to Poland, and we'd looked for the moon together. When it was still autumn, I'd carry him outside, but before I left in the early winter, we'd go to the back and front doors of our house, and, careful to keep him warm, I'd hold him in his sleeper next to the window and we'd look west and then east, searching for the moon, night-time to him being something between repetition and the completely new.

On Thursday, September 9, 1943, Mechanicus compared the half moon above Kamp Westerbork to a death mask: it was so pale it reminded him of Wilde's *Salome*. Only two days before, his friend, Etty Hillesum, had been sent east. None of those deported had any accurate sense of what this journey to Poland entailed. We now know that to go from Westerbork to Auschwitz-Birkenau usually took most of two days. It took longer to arrive at Sobibór.

Hillesum survived the selection. And only two weeks before, both of them, Etty (the name she preferred) and Mechanicus (similarly), had agonized about what it meant to (safely) watch the transport of

August 24, 1943. But on September 10, 1943, of the two of them, only she would have had an immediate sense of what Poland meant. The moon figures often in Etty's work, usually as a kind of metaphysical witness to the confusions of human experience. It signaled a kind of purity to her, and it was usually something she experienced when she was enjoying her solitude walking alongside Amsterdam's canals: she might have noticed the moon that Mechanicus wrote about that early September night.

Etty observed: "We have not yet gained a common sense of history."

The SS documented 987 "pieces" arriving from Westerbork on September 9, 1943. Only eight people from that specific RSHA transport of September 7 survived the Shoah. The point of historical memory is to gather disparate individual experience into something coeval that can be passed on. But of this or any other transport that left Westerbork: how could anyone on them know anything other than what happened to each of them individually? No one saw everything; no one could have seen what's required to be seen. Several thousand were living at Westerbork on November 30, 1943, but Mechanicus wrote all that remains of what happened there on that day, and he would never learn that the Red Cross recorded that Etty died that same Tuesday. We don't know the circumstances of her death. Any number of people would have surrounded her, whether she died jammed in a bunk at night of the typhus epidemic that fall, or with others in a gas chamber, or if she was killed by a Kapo because she mouthed off or disobeyed. She often complains about her feet in her diaries; survivors tell how damaged feet were amongst their greatest fears. To use the harsh argot of the camps, perhaps she'd croaked because she'd simply become unlucky with her feet.

Only two years earlier, Etty had gone skating in Amsterdam, and addressing "a few stupid remarks to the moon," she reminded herself that the moon had seen the likes of her before. And a hard life, she predicted, would await her. In the same diary entry, Etty wrote of her desire to "know this century of ours, inside and out… to run [her] fingers along the contours of our age." The question that won't go away is how she felt about those contours after she was forced to stop writing. We know she brought a notebook with her on the train; it would have been torn from her when she arrived. What happened to her between September 7 and November 30, and how she responded, is unknown. How did she judge her pre-Auschwitz self? What, precisely, does "our century" mean, especially for those of us who were formed by the twentieth century, yet entered it long after she wrote about such things on a day made both huge and tiny in 1941?

That she encapsulated Dada within a single paragraph, completely alone, knowing nothing of Zurich, Berlin, or Dresden. That she lived amongst death's indisputable entrances more than Heidegger could ever discover. That she was ignorant of Pessoa and Proust. Also of Simone Weil. That no one knows what she felt upon waking up on her first morning in the camp. Or her second day. The third day, also unique. When did she understand what had happened to her parents? That she would never learn what would happen to her schizophrenic brother Mischa. That to emphasize her death over the deaths of others would have been offensive to her. That she believed every life can be a lens, and she also knew that every time she wasn't sent away on a transport, someone else had to go in

her place. That to view her life
through Auschwitz   is to forget
the joyful _____ of words being formed
by a pen, any pen, though
                                        she
likely had a favourite in Amsterdam, one pen
which felt best in her fingers and made the sharpest cut in the letters
that makes
each word a separate bit of fun, holding the love and sometimes the fury

[I can't think of the right word, or phrase, to finish this sentence]

that is hers

alone. The love and fury, then, that took

place on her beloved desk.

A miracle you learn as a child: there's something in my head that no one else can see—

Etty Hillesum and Rainer Maria Rilke

Like many writers, especially those of her generation, Etty reacted to Rilke as though he was speaking directly to her. Initially he was her mentor, but then she trusted him enough to use him as a kind of flashlight that helped her explore what she couldn't make out by herself. In the spring of 1942 she wrote:

> Slowly but surely I have been soaking Rilke up these last few months: the man, his work, and his life. And that is probably the only right way with literature, with study, with people, or with anything else: to let it all soak in, to let it mature slowly inside you until it has become part of yourself.... And in between, emotions and sensations that strike you like lightning. But still the most important thing is the organic process of growing.

By the summer and certainly the autumn of that year, she'd gone from being a fan to becoming someone who'd earned an interiority that Rilke himself would have recognized.

To ask what might deserve Rilke's angels' attention points to an irresolvable anguish: how can anyone discern, let alone express, what's unique about the transitory? What's at stake has become almost simple: damage, irreparable damage has been done to what Rilke heard—when he cried out there—blessedly alone with the sky and sea immediately nearby. I don't think it's possible to inherit Rilke without Hillesum. To read her letter of August 24, 1943, in which she describes a transport being readied and then sent from Westerbork to a destination in Poland that no one inside one of those trains could comprehend upon hearing the doors fastened shut, is to recognize that her constrained agony is that slow and precise elegy that, in neglecting nothing, but settling nowhere,

completes Rilke's (ongoing) masterpiece. Is

what Etty felt necessary to show the angels, but only Etty and 986 other people were inside when their own transport doors were forced open on September 9, 1943.

Studying the Holocaust, you keep accidentally

discovering how incomprehensibly big... Etty receives only sentences in *The Holocaust Chronicle*, a book... 700 pages of text and photographs, intimates the blunt enormity... Mechanicus isn't... offsets the way your ignorance stares back... David Koker's diary that... fastidious (and particularly self-disciplined—though Koker couldn't have known these things) Heinrich Himmler[30] inspected Vught (near Amsterdam)... didn't recognize Westerbork in conversation, is... to be astonished that the "architect" of the Holocaust... unaware of its central Dutch... This paragraph unwillingly... this central paradox, but... remove it from a... ratio... isn't proportionate to... (unwillingly) describe as knowing... birch trees... Nazis keep inviting Hegel... suicide: Dariusz Jablonski's documentary of the first known... photographic slides... Himmler with the vanity licence plate SS 1.

For someone like me, who has no direct contact with the Holocaust, and speaks only

English, using my imagination to think about that life is as ethically complicated and as delusional as it's necessary. To explore Birkenau's ruins today is to sense how uneven the experience of the present is: everywhere is the unrelinquished and unjourneyed now.

Just over there is a replica of a guard tower that reinforces each kind of separation. What's here on these grounds is a loosely cluttered emptiness, and you can look at what's left of the women's barracks and wonder what Etty might have seen if she'd happened to stand in the same place. When, earlier that morning, I saw people pose in front of the *Arbeit Macht Frei* sign at Auschwitz, I was baffled. Much as I regret not having more photographs to use as notes now, I felt that to take a picture of that gate was far too immediate a response, and if to have a stranger point your phone or tablet at you and your partner seemed to me (a man who has always been safe) as possibly a moral travesty, what mostly stopped me from taking a

---

30   On May 18, 1942, Himmler stood in the back of a car in Amsterdam's Museumplein to address a newly formed brigade of Dutch police. It's technically possible that Etty saw him that rainy day: all she would have needed to do was walk a few steps from her door. No one today can say whether she did. We do know, though, that something was greatly disturbing her that day since her diary entry records an almost frantic effort to retain self-control. "The threat grows ever greater," she observes, "and terror increases from day to day."

picture of the gate was the excitement of being overwhelmed, of having time itself hurrying me past everything with such speed that it was impossible to notice anything, let alone take a picture of it.

 Walking with the past's unknowable violence safely blurred in my head, it was too soon to take pictures. And yet, at the end of my second afternoon at Birkenau, I found myself peering through a knothole in one of the wooden barracks before focusing my camera's viewfinder through it so that the endless immensity of leftover chimneys was there as if an actual *terra incognita*. If I hoped that this photo embodied the tension between what exists and the amplitude of what's missing, I also knew that I was responding to something that I'd seen before: those reflections in Dutch still-life paintings, often of a window steadily afloat in a beer glass or bowl holding flowers, those reflections intimating a shimmery world that's simultaneous with, yet beyond, the visual. Many of the buildings in Auschwitz have now been converted to national exhibits. Inside the building devoted to Poland, looking at some of the photographs (most of which I'd never seen before), I was surprised when my right hand suddenly covered my mouth (an involuntary motion that I first experienced in that room but have subsequently observed in other people on three occasions: a photo of a woman on Obama's team watching a screen and reacting to footage of special forces precisely when they killed Osama bin Laden; a picture of a child immediately after the Sandy Hook shootings; and then, in an artist's courtroom drawing of a recent serial killer being confronted with evidence of his crimes). I don't know what it means to be confronted with this gesture; I don't know how to distinguish between the atavistic and the particular. Let me put this problem, initially, like this: for Western culture, the idea of Auschwitz often serves as a kind of vague, though immediately recognizable (and perhaps *beguiling*), symbol of ultimate evil; though to walk on the word's actual grounds is to meet something that demands that everything one's known must change. But I don't understand how to articulate those demands, let alone meet them; I didn't know how to turn the slow movements of my feet on what's mostly a kind of gravel path there into a vague

recognition that there's an endless exactitude of loss. Those buildings that once held people   are still here.

A comet returned almost each week at Westerbork: each time a transport was prepared every *dinsdag* became a sag in the human experience of ongoing time. Put very differently, Etty refers to a blind man being shot because he strayed too close to the fence surrounding Westerbork.

Excerpts from Breslauer's film exist in at least three locations: the Internet, the Dutch exhibit at Auschwitz, and the Westerbork museum. If you can, travel to each place: each viewing of the movie requires something different from the person looking at it because the sound of the train picking up speed cleaves that day from every (successive) present.

Esther Hillesum, Philip Mechanicus

are names you can pick out of over a hundred thousand painted on a long wall in the building at Auschwitz that's been devoted to Dutch people the Nazis killed. But you have to look carefully to find those you're seeking, because they're in such a dense thicket of letters; no, that's not right. It's not a thicket. That the names painted there on the wall waver in a kind of silent pulse.

Hilversum, Hijman 16-5-1901 Amersfoort 3-11-1942
is far less than a finger's touch away from Hillesum, Esther
15-1-1914 Middelburg 30-11-1943

& Aristotle initiates one of his inquiries by

noting that it's through vision that people most delight in knowing—
 —Have I said it before? I am learning to see. Yes, I am beginning. It's still going badly. But I intend to make the most of my time.
 —I had to see everything. I had to watch hour after hour, by day and by night, the removal and burning of the bodies, the extraction of the teeth, the cutting of the hair, the whole grisly, interminable business… I had to stand for hours on end… I had to look through the peephole

of the gas chambers and watch the process of death itself, because the doctors wanted me to see it.

—I look around me: incapacity to experience the present. This coolness, this thinness, this calm and collected busyness. Our eyes are turned inward. Our visual faculty is unequal to the reality we inhabit. There ought to be something in us that makes us realize the image becomes permanent the moment we take it in. Right now it is thin, fluid, might just as well not be there.

—At Auschwitz and Birkenau themselves, the truth is there for all to see, and to see is better [*sic*] to understand.

Rilke. Höss. Koker. Greenman.

Greenman's wife Else & his son Barni were wearing

clothes that she'd sewn from velvet curtains, red capes that he could make out from a distance in the truck beneath a searchlight that separated them from the others

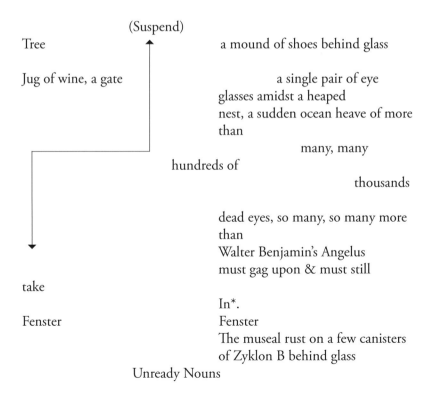

(Suspend)

Tree   a mound of shoes behind glass

Jug of wine, a gate   a single pair of eye
glasses amidst a heaped
nest, a sudden ocean heave of more
than
                              many, many
hundreds of
                                  thousands

dead eyes, so many, so many more
than
Walter Benjamin's Angelus
must gag upon & must still

take
                 In*.
Fenster   Fenster
                  The museal rust on a few canisters
                  of Zyklon B behind glass
             Unready Nouns

*The Paul Klee drawing Benjamin once owned—its precise child-like warning/accusation only clear when you see it watching you across from a piece of old and very ordinary, slightly browned paper—was on display in Boston's Museum of Fine Arts from the summer of 2012 to early January 2013 as part of the Ori Gersht exhibit. Presumably, the Angel had been returned to its glass case in Jerusalem when two bombs went off in the Boston Marathon only a few months later.

Paradise: the response given by Wilfred von Oven, Josef Goebbels's personal assistant, upon being asked, in 1990, how he might summarize his experience of the Third Reich in one word.

The aura that's still here retains

a silent, though clear, almost concussive directive, ordering people to *submit*. The buildings and paths take on the characteristics of a malevolent Being that only permits you to be there because it is being forced to.

There's a metal noose identifying where Kommandant Höss was hanged in 1947, but I didn't take a photograph of it: I should have stood and looked at it for a while, but I didn't because everything about it seemed beside the point, and yet to know of his execution would have shifted everything within his Lager: for inmates to imagine themselves standing there, alive, and seeing him sentenced to dangle. Not far from the scaffold, I looked up into the windows of the building in which medical experiments had been performed, and then I started to head back to the gate when I heard thunder. I was getting close to the open grass where it's likely Mechanicus was shot in 1944, and I asked myself: what did it mean for inmates to hear something from their previous lives that was as normal and exhilarating as thunder is? Did it even register for them? How? How could they comprehend what was on the other side of what was completely *away*, was entirely separate from them?

If she was incarcerated in the women's camp at Birkenau, Etty would have seen

trucks from transports roll in, but she wouldn't have arrived on the central track tourists such as myself see at Birkenau, which wasn't built (until after) when she arrived from Westerbork. As with Greenman, the train on which she'd travelled would have stopped some distance from Birkenau, and she would have seen just about everyone taken away in trucks, while she marched to the camp.

An email written to SL from Amsterdam on Wednesday, November 16, 2011:

Have walked around quite a bit today beneath lovely grey skies, bits of rain, first the Rijksmuseum, and then just general flânerie, a chat with my wife, and did my laundry; nice to have fresh clothes when you're travelling. Then walked around some more. It makes sense that the Dutch started NYC becos the two cities seem to have much in common in terms of their odd light, general sort of free-for-all on the streets, and tolerant excess.

Yesterday I rented a car and drove to Kamp Westerbork, but I won't describe it just now except to say that there's a museum re: Nazism (attended yesterday by a class of school children caught up in their own games), but then you need to walk a little under 4km to get to the camp. You follow a zigzaggy brick path amidst this most beautiful forest, and all along the walkway are these enormous discoloured green satellite dishes lined up in the clearings, and pictures [along the walkway] showing the universe because this area is where Holland has its largest gatherings of radio telescopes. So here's a snapshot of our species: the way we educate our young, the 1940s, and we reach to discover more about the universe: tell me about this creature responsible for all of these things.

Something that was unexpected is how beautiful these places are in the autumn. I went to Auschwitz twice, and both times was in Birkenau at dusk, which comes early amidst enormous trees, some of which must have been there when the camp was in use. At one point during my first afternoon there, it thundered, and it took me a moment to realize it was thundering because I've always associated such weather with a mood of quiet excitement, joy. Thunder didn't feel normal there.

Something that surprised me: people have put cigarette butts in the small stoves in the surviving barracks, and there are dozens of names carved into the wooden walls and bunks. (Note: these aren't from the 1940s; they're from recent tourists.)

Such a change, then, to come to Amsterdam and look at Rembrandt, Vermeer, Steen. Looking at paintings, the retina takes an undiluted image straight to the brain, but the brain doesn't have to subdue what the eye sees, filter it, and then somehow re-imagine, somehow overlay what's directly in front of you with what's missing as it does in Auschwitz or Westerbork. I spent a long time looking at a simple picture Rembrandt made of an old woman reading, and he devotes all of his genius to painting her wrinkled, aging hand that's resting on the enormous book. I bought a plastic reproduction, but it can't convey the paper feel of her almost gecko/like skin. There: in front of yr eyes, is something he made only a few centuries ago. I don't think I've ever seen any representation that more fully embodies the human than her hand.

It's very strange, then, to leave these paintings and walk south on the Museumplein for a few minutes to Gabriël Metsustraat 6, which is where Etty lived during part of the war. There's a plaque at street level identifying this place as her residence, but the dates it gives, oddly, are incorrect. She once wrote about looking out her window toward the Rijksmuseum, which, in the mist, seemed to be a "turreted city far away." But the plaque's all that's there now—unlike the Anne Frank Huis, this row house is still someone's home—and I didn't notice anyone stop to read what was written there alongside the doorway.

Warmly to you, from that other city with canals.

P.S. Find attached a photo taken at Westerbork yesterday.

Today, I turned a corner in Amsterdam's Joods Historisch Museum and unexpectedly saw some notebooks in a glass case. There were only five of them, but I sensed immediately that they must have been Etty's. Because there were no identifying labels, I couldn't be sure until I finally found a computer display that worked and touched the icon that identified the stack of ringed notebooks as being hers.

On August 31, 1943, the Tuesday before Etty's transport, Mechanicus recorded how "loathsome" it was that ballet dancers were ordered to rehearse their routine for an upcoming theatrical show while that week's transport was being readied and then sent east, Gemmeker having committed 2,000 guilders to pay for costumes—

HOME IS WHAT TRAVELS
THROUGH US

ZEN AND A DINOSAUR

Home is what travels through us.

*

Jakob had just come upstairs to show me a drawing he'd made of a shark. When he's not drawing, he's writing. He knows all sorts of statistics regarding the bite force of the various apex carnivores that populate his stories. After we spoke about the shark, which was actually a hybrid between a great white and a vampire—the fins are folded across the shark's chest like Dracula asleep in his coffin—I returned to what I'd been reading: Janwillem van de Wetering's *The Empty Mirror*, a memoir of the time he'd spent in a Zen monastery in Kyoto as a young man. The book had recently arrived in the mail from Amazon, but the first time I'd read it was about a year after it was published in 1973. I'd borrowed it from the public library in New Hamburg, the small town in southern Ontario where I grew up.

*

I've decided to approach Buddhism again because my mood disorders won't abate: picture an open window with a soft, translucent curtain. When the wind blows, the curtain turns toward me however-many times during a day: the curtain noiselessly moving this way may as well be the sudden, mostly unexpected, moment when anxiety enters my psyche, utterly absorbing it. Inside it, inside this room that anxiety makes inside me, a mantra enters my mind at least a dozen times a day, usually more: *keep them safe*, them being Amy and the kids, safe from everything from a car accident to ecological disaster. Just as tinnitus has made it impossible for me to take refuge in silence ever again, anxiety is always either here or threatening to arrive from somewhere. Is it here for the duration of my life, will it worsen, or will meditation help put it to rest?

*

While there are parts of the Van de Wetering memoir I remember, there was nothing familiar about the particular scene I'd been reading when Jakob came into the room: Van de Wetering was trying to control his anger after being rebuked by a master while working in the monastery's garden. What's impossible for me to grasp is that, between my first and second time encountering the sentences in this book, more than forty years have passed. What I'd like to know now is what my younger self would think if he'd been able to look up from the library book in his hands and have loose access to the man he'd somehow become. If I could have him shift from that long-gone fraying chair (in his bedroom because it was no longer needed by a deteriorating grandparent) to the one in this room in Saskatchewan, a chair that came from IKEA, what would he think?

After doing a quick mental probe, he'd immediately ascertain that he hadn't become enlightened. How was this possible? What had interfered with those plans to emulate Van de Wetering and go to Japan immediately after completing high school and stay there until achieving satori, something that, according to the memoir, the young Dutch man had (inexplicably) failed to accomplish? But before he, the younger me that is, could register disappointment in his spiritual state, remove the bad taste from his mouth, he would have to take in that he'd become a father, and did the child's very long, blond hair mean that his mother was Scandinavian?

Looking around the busy sunroom, this younger self would see that books have remained important. There are hundreds of them, on shelves and piled on the floor. Literature (poetry mostly); others on ecology, art history, philosophy; five or six concerning addiction; and an entire bookcase devoted to the Holocaust. Art postcards on the walls, binoculars on the desk facing a wall of windows, and a large photograph of a woman's bare feet with the words *welcome home* painted on her toes. A stationary bicycle. Oddly, a few Polaroids. That both rooms are painted the same yellow is uncanny (not that he'd use this word): on the one hand, it feels exactly right, but, on the other, it's slightly disturbing: don't one's tastes change or develop over time?

Instead of the large classical Buddha statue he'd once owned, there's a very small one almost entirely obscured by a tarantula fern. Also a small Bodhisattva, painted with what appears to be pink nail polish. No plastic milk carton storing LP records. And what's with the antique dolls? A half of a lemon that seems mummified nestles beside a cactus, and stranger still, a few things inside Ziploc bags are taped against a wall: what's left of a flower (he wouldn't know it's a five-year-old souvenir from an evening stroll down Nieuwe Keizersgracht in Amsterdam); the darkening claws of a bird that once struck a window. A finely detailed toy camel has been cut in half in its middle, and both parts glued to the wall. If you look at the back part of its torso, it appears as if the animal has exited from the house, but at the same time, only a finger's width away, the neck and head, forefeet in mid-stride, have just emerged seemingly from another dimension on the other side of the wall and entered the room again.

And yes, there it is: what's now a very old scar, left over from when, only the week before the teenager had started reading the Van de Wetering, he'd lit a match and watched it burn out on the skin of his left hand. There are other scars about whose origin he won't know. There was no Internet when he was in *his/my* early twenties, so he had to discover cutting on his own. There once had been a few case cutters left over from working nights in a grocery store.

*

The teenager's Buddha statue only exists in the photograph to my left, an image showing a slightly shattered statue in an open suitcase. My father was de-cluttering and he decided to bring me the statue that I'd stored with him, but packed it with socks and underwear, and then had it go through normal luggage on a flight from Ontario about five years ago. Now there's a concrete instance of the transitory nature of reality. To me, the photo is a finely compressed detail that speaks of Dad slowing down, being inattentive, and the picture is also a goofy setting for this statue, one that could even stimulate its own koan: instead of concentrating on the face you had before you were born, hold the thought of a fairly shattered Buddha in a suitcase along with the socks and underwear of a seventy-six year-old and see what this tells you about emptiness and its vicissitudes.

*

Wikipedia tells me that Van de Wetering died over a decade ago, as a man nearing eighty in 2008. After publishing the book on Zen in the 1970s, he'd made a career writing detective fiction, eventually leaving the Netherlands for the States, though he did revisit his youthful sojourn in Kyoto, turning out another memoir in 1999, this one called *Afterzen*. From it and an interview online, I've learned that one of the reasons he initially turned to Zen was his confusion over suffering and evil: only after the war did he learn that the teenage boys who had disappeared from his school in Rotterdam had died at Treblinka. I also learned that booze had been a decades-long companion until his wife put her foot down. When I'd originally read Van de Wetering, he was in his early 40s, and he had over thirty books yet to write. Apparently, he'd maintained his meditation practice more or less and practised in the proximity of a small altar he'd made, decorating it with Dutch sea shells to remind him of his childhood and also some plastic dinosaurs to keep the idea of extinction directly in front of him. I've never gotten much out of detective fiction, but I'm half tempted to order one of his mystery novels. Someone who decorates a homemade altar with a toy dinosaur is likely to be good at nestling surprising details inside his fiction: small gems that coalesce around how the world appears perhaps only to him.

*

A red-breasted nuthatch has just flown off with a sunflower seed from the feeder two stories below. I put out seeds all year, even during the summer. The bird may be the one who waits for me in the early morning when I replenish the feeder. Often we'll look at each other, only an arm's length apart. Almost all birds appeal to me, but I've wondered for years why this specific species gives me a particular dopamine rush. It's precognitive: as soon as I even remotely register the grey-blue feathers of the bird, its eye stripe and black beak, it seems as though my hypothalamus is flooded with not only simple equanimity, but euphoria as well. For years now, I've wondered why one of these small creatures triggers these emotions. I'm unsure, but through meditation, I think that I may be getting closer to the cause. Feelings are bizarre. If they seem to arrive as contemporaries of the present, a reaction to immediate circumstances, they may in fact be very ancient, far older than anything we can consciously identify.

I'm lousy at meditating and suspect that decades of anxiety (among other things) have torpedoed the tissues in my brain… but here's the thing: back when I was reading *The Empty Mirror* and planning on travelling to Kyoto, I used to take long winter walks along a nearby frozen river, hike through the forest that followed its contours. Recently, during sessions of regular, extraordinarily difficult, breathing exercises, I've found that unusual images suddenly veer toward my unanchored mind, some bizarre—Michael Jackson's face during plastic surgery shot by on one occasion—but others seeming to arrive from my own deep past, showing memories that have been lost for decades. Sitting on a dock as a child about to try waterskiing for the first time, the waves making my feet move up and down, everything as if filmed by a parent, but ordinary people didn't have the technology to record anything back then like we do now. Gene Simmons spitting blood on a stage the one time I saw KISS. Eventually, a recollection from one of those walks along the forest by the river came into view. In it, snow is everywhere, deeper than my knees, and thick tufts of it are on the trees. In this memory, I watch myself stop walking and turn around to look behind. There's a bit of snow falling from some kind of pine tree. A grey sky. I can't say for certain, but upon repeated viewings of this scene when I've been observing breaths for a half hour or so, I've wondered whether I didn't turn around because I heard the singular sound that a long-dead white-breasted nuthatch once might have made. And within that sound, I felt a sense of well-being that nestled somewhere inside and then seemingly vanished beneath the subsequent decades that came next. I'll never know for certain if there actually was a nuthatch (though I do know that I have to struggle to keep references to snow out of the poetry I write). And I know that birds aren't here to provide us with spiritual sustenance. It's simply that some things went right in my life after those moments in the snow, many things went right, and other, different things began to occur very shortly after reading Van de Wetering, some habits that distracted me from the ambition to travel to Japan.

*

But what's staying with me now is a detail of which I have no recollection from my first reading of Van de Wetering's story. The ship that took him to Japan docked briefly in Bombay, where he went ashore to be surrounded by beggars, their number surprising him. "The hunger we knew in Holland during the winter of 1944-45," he says, "seemed to be a normal and permanent phenomenon here [in Bombay]." While ashore, a sailor tells him about a brothel where women are kept in cages, and to his credit, Van de Wetering caustically asks whether it would make any difference to either the beggars or these women whether a clever young man managed to gain enlightenment after spending a year or so in a monastery. I note that he doesn't call these caged sex workers *prostitutes*, but the Dutch word translated into English tells me that he thought of these people as *women*. I don't have the slightest inkling of what this passage meant to me when I first read it. Van de Wetering had these temporary misgivings in 1958, en route to Kyoto, and eventually I read and then forgot about them during the 1970s, but today, I can't help but wonder whether any of these people, peripheral to the memoir, are still alive today, more than sixty years after that stop in Bombay.

Imagine the trajectory of their lives. If we're honest, we'll admit we can't. To ask what happened to *only one* of the beggars that Van de Wetering saw or stood next to is to recognize the vastness of oblivion and that almost all human experience is evanescent and cruelly unknowable. I don't know how to confront this fact, except to put it like this: while I was burning incense, reading *The Empty Mirror* for the first time, listening to Deep Purple's *Machine Head*, and going for walks in the snow, I had no idea that the Khmer Rouge was beginning its policy of genocide in Cambodia.

Contained in a heavy cardboard box, Ben Kiernan's history of the Pol Pot regime has recently arrived, and this is one of the books my previous self would have noticed if I'd been able to transport him from the first reading of Van de Wetering to the second. But I have no sense as to what reading the Kiernan will actually mean when I finally find the time to start the book. I've been to Auschwitz, Mauthausen, Westerbork, and Dachau. I'm fairly certain that I'll never go to Cambodia's killing fields.

*

Time baffles me. I simply cannot understand how one day passes into another. For years now, I've thought that time is the most mysterious of our experiences, but now I understand that being a parent means having to acknowledge something even more perplexing: to bring a birth is also to bring one more death into the world.

*

According to Armstrong™ (Canada's Premiere Bird Food), its product named *Persistence* (a blend of quality seeds, nuts, and dried fruits, including pineapple) is "wild bird food for woodpeckers, nuthatches, and other *hardworking birds*" [my emphasis]. Neoliberalism in bed with John Calvin.

*

A few facts and questions that must interrupt this essay:

1. My blond son's mother isn't Scandinavian; her heritage is Ashkenazi.
2. When I was a child, I could make snow forts out of what was left after a plow went down the road, and these forts would be higher than my father. My sister (who still lives in the area) tells me that there's rarely any snow on the hills where we used to go tobogganing in the winter. It rains more than it snows. She puts it down to global warming.
3. Before this past early spring, a catbird had never visited our backyard, but today, one has. Using my binoculars, I follow this new

arrival as he searches for seeds… the black, grey, and red on his body summon something deeper than ink, a sky of the thickest rain, and a piece of red felt that's rarely seen.

4. Jakob has two large overflowing plastic boxes of dinosaurs tumbled in disarray, each toy a perfect replica of a specific species: a large collection of plastic toys made of polymers that have made the long journey from China to his bedroom.

5. Jakob doesn't know about refugees dying in the Sahara or children walking from Guatemala to the United States, but one day he'll be forced to confront the reality that while he's been writing stories about dinosaurs, Joy the Murderous Clown, and also before, when he was teaching himself how to draw by creating hybrid sharks, another extinction has been happening—in the oceans and rain forests that are so far from the Canadian prairies; and everywhere else too, including Saskatchewan's grasslands—and there's nothing he can do about it. *Extinction* is a word no one can accurately understand: it may be an indifferent volcano; we might force ourselves to its rim, but who has the courage to look down into what's beyond the edge?

6. Will Jakob know food insecurity in his old age, as Van de Wetering experienced in his childhood?

7. How will Jakob eventually remember the climate strikes we went to when he was eight, nine, and ten?

8. Can anyone doubt that our children will look back on us with incomprehension and likely a long-abiding sense of contempt?

9. Dinosaurs once were real and knew nothing of us, and we've put them in movies and museums, but what's most important today is that together we've made fossil fuels.

10.

MAY TO JUNE 2020… A COVID MISCELLANY

Saturday, May 2

Nurses love the word *perfect*: as in, do you know what day it is? *Per*fect.

Also, *scoot*: I'm just going to *scoot* you over there to the other side of the bed, when a patient fouls herself and needs to be bathed. No worries, the nurse tells her, I do poop, but not vomit. Francine does vomit. Each nurse pushes the lever on the hand sanitizer on the wall upon leaving the room, and each one remarks that it's still empty.

It seems unaccountably stupid that I'm in the General Hospital while the world is being devastated by COVID.

Tequila + chronic depression and generalized anxiety + new and unfamiliar meds → my own private ecological catastrophe. I'm having what used to be called *a nervous breakdown* and now I need to be kept under observation for several days.

Don't get me wrong, this collapse was a long time coming.

My voice is barely intelligible.

Sunday, May 3

I experience *déjà vu* the very second the physiotherapist mentions he wants to get a Fitbit to track how many steps he takes in a day.

I'm told that there don't seem to be any long-term medical consequences related to my admittance, and I want to go home, but I'm told that I'm going to be transferred to the mental health unit. *What if, as an adult, I refuse to go?* I ask. *Then we have to have you committed.*

Monday, May 4

An announcement on the intercom wakes me up: *Code Blue on the Heliport.* Chairs scrape out in the hall. People rush. When they hear these words, do staff first picture the colour, or does the message's urgency overrule the way each person summons blue?

The man in the bed beside mine is 84, but suddenly turned blind when he was 21. Upon the delivery of food in the morning, he keeps calling out *I can't find my breakfast* because the nurse's aide put it in a different place than before.

David Foster Wallace's *Infinite Jest* is the perfect reading material while I'm here. The first time I read it a few years ago, I was also in a deplorable state. I put the book down for my daily ECG.

Tuesday, May 5

A string of dental floss, the nurse in the psych ward handing it to me, my own supply confiscated in case I tried to use it to perform self-harm. The psychiatrist refuses to let me go home.

A woman walks by whose bare feet look like they've been hacked out of an El Greco painting.

Wednesday, May 6

Each morning upon waking, I'm given a blood test, and then three times throughout the day my blood pressure is taken. Meds come in a small paper cup to be taken with water in a Dixie cup. Just like in the movies, the nurse looks directly at me until I've swallowed the pills.

I'm reminded of the twentieth century because when someone walks by speaking aloud it's because he's mentally ill, not because he's wearing a Bluetooth.

A fellow in what's called *Group* (a circle of people sitting across from each other in a small room) is bipolar, and what he most wants to do is rub ropes of wool in his hands, pet them, because he is *feeling very sensitive* and the wool is soft and soothing to the touch. Another fellow bursts into tears as he recalls fishing with his father and brother, and when the session is over he asks the leader for a hug—but of course COVID denies that.

There is a small personal benefit to COVID: my germophobia doesn't look unusual to anyone; it appears that I'm merely doing what's recommended by washing my hands so often.

Thursday, May 7

I'm discharged. Following the nurse to the locked door, I realize I've not been outside for nearly an entire week. A messy man approaches from the parking lot as I wait for Amy to pick me up. He wants me to buy some art he's made—stick people shaded in various colours and two fire engines—but I tell him truthfully I have no money. *How long have you been in there?* he asks, nodding at the exit from the Mental Health Wing. *That's a hard place to get out of,* he says, moving away as a security guard approaches to warn him off hospital property.

Robert Hass always startles me in his poem "Consciousness" when he claims a father's duty is to teach his children how to die properly. In the evening, Jesse and I go for a walk, and I partially explain what happened. Only days before, he turned 21. We pass by places we went sledding in his childhood. He listens with decency and compassion: I'm a lucky man who doesn't deserve his care.

His father and my own, my father's father too: men with any number of weaknesses, each of us unable to sustain a first marriage.

Saturday, May 9

I finish Albert Camus's *The Plague*. Originally published in 1947, the novel was meant to allegorize the Nazi occupation, though it's startlingly prescient of COVID. "What's natural is the microbe," Camus writes, of the plague-ridden city of Oran.

One character refers to a criminal he'd seen in court many years earlier and says that he "looked like a yellow owl scared blind by too much light." A few pages earlier, the reader will have come across these words: "In fact, it comes to this: nobody is capable of thinking about anyone."

Monday, May 11

Who will be resuscitated today?

Tuesday, May 12

Only weeks ago, enraged Brazilians stood on their balconies and beat large spoons against pots and pans to protest their president's inept and callous response to the virus.

When Britain's lockdown began, a woman with Alzheimer's (who has responded to her condition by discussing the disease at symposia and hospitals all over England for the past few years) blogs her fear that her dementia will worsen because she's no longer able to experience the mental stimulation travel provides.

Thursday, May 14

Jakob (10 this year) and I have been going for walks most mornings around Wascana Lake, our binoculars hanging around our necks, to view birds along the lake. The ones he's got were originally mine; I bought them when I was fourteen with money I earned shoveling snow and cutting grass. The Snowbird jets pass overhead, flying east and then west over Regina; their purpose ostensibly is to lift people's spirits because of COVID. Heading for the trees, we stay off the path, which has signs advising people to walk around the lake clockwise to practice social distancing.

Some twenty minutes later, we hear and then see the first male Baltimore oriole of the season, the bright orange of his plumage the colour of an incandescent plastic pumpkin, the sort kids carry on Halloween for their candy. Jakob has never seen this bird species before. He wonders if we'll still be in lockdown when Halloween comes. And then he says that Halloween this year will special: there will be a full moon on the 31st.

Time has always obsessed me in its existential glare, especially when I think of all that has happened on certain special days. But now, my concern about time is simpler: it's panic about the future. I can't help myself from asking Google when the next full moon will occur on Halloween. 2039. If I make it, I'll be almost eighty, and Jakob will be at the end of his twenties. Given that 2020 is looking to be the hottest year on record, what will his world be like in the face of global warming? Will there be another pandemic between now and then? One that is more lethal?

Today is Dad's 81st birthday.

He's had a chair installed that will take him up the staircase from the main floor to his bedroom: cheaper, and safer he says, than going into a nursing home.

Sunday, May 17

One of the Snowbirds crashes in Kamloops, killing 2 people. Standing near the dirty kitchen sink, Amy and I discuss whether we should let Jakob know about this accident: being unable to go to school or play with his friends has weighed down his spirits.

Monday, May 18

Roger and Brian Eno's album *Mixing Colours*, a decade and a half in the making, has been available online for 27 days. Most of the selections attempt to render colour in music: just now, I'm listening to "Verdigris." About 50 seconds into the video featuring "Obsidian," two birds in the distance fly across a river, their movement going from the right part of the screen to the left in opposition to the camera pan that moves from left to right and seems to be filmed from a railway bridge. Perhaps these dark birds are meant to evoke obsidian in this video that seems to have been filmed through roving mist.

The graphic novel of Norse mythology I've ordered online for Jakob still hasn't arrived.

COVID is gaining momentum in the U.S. (over 70,000 deaths), but cases are low in South Korea (under 300). South Korea paid attention to SARS. Derek Thompson observes: "The truth is that the Korean government and its citizens did something simple, admirable, and all too rare: They suffered from history, and they learned from it."

Suffered from history: in 1980, May 18 was a Sunday, and in South Korea troops fired on students, marking the Gwangju Massacre; across the ocean at the very same time, Mount St. Helens blew the day apart, lava and ash covering Harry Truman and his 16 cats, Harry a former World War I pilot who refused to budge from the place he made his own on Spirit Lake. And many dead students were lying in a perfectly straight line because that's how they fell.

Because history sometimes wears riding spurs to bed, and at the same time its swirling ash pounds bullet holes into the ecology of a day's deranged and vanishing architecture.

Tuesday, May 19

Five turkey vultures make sweeping circles overhead. Apart from American pelicans, the rare eagle, no other bird soars with such majesty over southern Saskatchewan. Something invisible in the messy sky has opened and let them through.

Wednesday, May 20

Woden's day.

An electronic billboard on Albert Street announces: *If there was no change, there wouldn't be any butterflies.*

Umm, OK.

And from Walpola Rahula's *What the Buddha Taught*:

The conception of *dukkha* may be viewed from three aspects: (1) *dukkha* as ordinary suffering (*dukkha-dukkha*), (2) *dukkha* as produced by change (*viparināma-dukkha*) and *dukkha* as conditioned states (*samkhāra-dukkha*).

Which means we don't own anything, especially our health, but it doesn't mean we shouldn't be attentive to daily instances of the flamboyant.

What would my life have been like had I understood these notions when I first read them after finding this book in a secondhand bookstore in Hamilton when our high school track club had gone there for an indoor track meet? The obvious answer, no less meaningful for being obvious, is that I *couldn't* have understood them, not at that time.

My niece, a nurse who has been deployed in a care home, has tested positive for COVID. She needs to self-quarantine in her apartment for two weeks.

I can still recall the bad air and the banging sound of runners when they came around the raised wooden curves of the track.

May 20 always makes me think of R. because it's her birthday. I proposed to her and then backed off a few months later in the summer of 1984. Hidden by the understory of trees in Toronto's High Park, we had sex for the final time.

Thursday, May 21
Thor's day.

Today two items came in the mail: a bill for the ambulance that came on May 1 and Gareth Hinds's ingenious graphic novel of Edgar Allan Poe's writing.

The first story is "The Masque of the Red Death."

Because he's been kept from school, Jakob and I have been reading much of Hinds's work. Strange that Poe doesn't dwell on what I consider the strangest of experiences: the passing of time. Recent studies in addiction suggest that addicts like Poe are entombed in the present, being incapable of mediating the present with an ongoing "life narrative" that conjoins the past, present, and future.

$325 for the ambulance, but what of those who couldn't afford this bill, or those for whom no ambulance comes at all?

When I played Jakob "The Raven" from the Alan Parsons Project debut album *Tales of Mystery and Imagination* (1976), he said it was "all right, but not [his] favourite." He far prefers the drawing Hinds made of the bird with figures of skulls and bony claws almost hidden in its plumage.

Friday, May 22
Friya's day.

Amy and Jakob go on their bi-weekly cat run, driving to about seven outdoor shelters to put out food and water for feral cats.

An email from Mom, subject heading *Well, another friend gone*:

Sandra had been at Chartwell nursing home for a few years and did very well, always busy. The last couple weeks before Covid 19 we noticed she was forgetting things. Then Covid......... Ken [her deceased husband] had come back and she was so mixed up but didn't really realize how mixed up she was, then couldn't do anything herself. It was heartbreaking to watch her deteriorate. Management told Julie this happened to a lot of residents as they were ALONE in rooms for weeks.

Eventually, after severe weight loss, deterioration in every manner she had what they thought was a stroke and peacefully stopped breathing in hospital Tuesday.

Unfortunately, no public funeral no saying goodbye to a very special friend for many years.

Who still reads the diary of *Blutodrdensträger* Felix Landau, a member of an *Einsatzkommando*, a Nazi who is mostly known for employing Bruno Schulz to paint murals in his son's room? From his diary written just over seventy-nine years ago today:

One hour later, at 5 in the morning, a further thirty-two Poles, members of the Intelligentsia and Resistance, were shot about two hundred meters from our quarters after they had dug their own grave. One of them simply would not die. The first layer of sand had already been thrown on the first group when a hand emerged from the sand, waved and pointed to a place, presumably his heart. A couple more shots rang out, then someone shouted—in fact, the Pole himself—"Shoot faster!" *What is a human being?*

Saturday, May 22

Three weeks ago I awoke in the ICU, and today Amy and I argue about sharing domestic chores. She's right: she does more around the house than I do. That doesn't stop me from furiously sulking as I clean the bathroom from ceiling to floor.

"Is every moment morally significant?" asks Iris Murdoch in *Metaphysics as a Guide to Morals*. The unavoidable question is: at what stage was her incipient Alzheimer's disease when she wrote this late book, extraordinary for its clarity? Its erudition gathered over a lifetime of reading. Its capacity for exploring what she describes as the "weirdness of being human."

To bring something new into the world. My mind isn't right. Auschwitz-Birkenau. Hang-gliding. Now: to hang-glide into Auschwitz. Obscenity and revelation.

Sunday, May 24, 2020
The self is not the subject of memoir… but its instrument. And the work of the self is not to "narrate" but to describe.

Patricia Hampl, "The Dark Art of Description"

Monday, May 25
Jakob has become very blue because of COVID isolation and my stay in the hospital.

Desperate to shift his mood, Amy has taken him to get some donuts and then to the railway bridge where he can shoot cherry pits into the creek below with his new slingshot. Two trains, the first coming out of the blur and going west, the other east, take them utterly by surprise. And then afterwards, a cop in a ghost car shows up, wanting to know if they've seen kids playing on the tracks. *No*, she says, telling me later she's never lied to a police officer before.

Gilles Deleuze advises that we should "become worthy of what happens to us." How is one supposed to do this, exactly?

I watched *What Dreams May Come*, starring Robin Williams as a husband and father in the afterlife. His character's name is Christy. Hmmm, the workaday profundity of Hollywood. Popular culture follows Dante in placing suicides in hell. One of the damned, buried up to his face in *What Dreams May Come*, is Werner Herzog, who mistakes Christy for one of his own children who never visit dear old Dad among thousands similarly positioned, each looking skyward, though there's no earthly sky above. Did Williams ponder his character's role when he killed himself by asphyxia in 2014?

Wednesday, May 27
The Sunday *New York Times* arrives. The entire first page (along with the pages 12-14) lists thousands of names of Americans who have died of COVID, and it also gives a brief description of their lives: **Dante Dennis Flagello**, *62, Rome, Ga., his greatest accomplishment was his relationship with his wife.*

Change.org has just sent an email asking subscribers to sign a petition protesting an online company that sells baby turtles encased in resin to be used as paperweights. Online shoppers have an interest in paperweights?

Thursday, May 28

At dusk Amy found a weakened bumblebee resting on a garden stepping stone. She'd heard that sugar water can energize them, so she put a small amount in the lid from an empty canister of hot chocolate and spooned it toward the bee. She'd poured the sugar from a glass container with a metal spout, the sort retro diners use.

I don't feel entirely present. It's as though when I look at what's in front of me there's a narrow, vertical band of something missing off to the right. Picture a long, straight line of light, but the line isn't made of light so much as it's a shaft of non-colour, non-presence, as though something on the other side of what's visible has sucked away the space holding whatever this line is.

It's difficult to fathom, but I spoke with someone on the street who believes that Trump is right and COVID is most likely a hoax.

Michel Pastoureau's sullenly beautiful *Yellow: The History of a Color* is dropped off in our mailbox even though I ordered it only days ago:

Some yellows are fortifying and joyous, but others are not. It is enough to apply them lightly over green or beige, to surround them with somber or pallid colors, or to employ them in a more or less empty space to convey a feeling of anguish, sadness or abandonment. The famous painting by Edward Hopper (1882–1957) titled *Automat*, portraying a woman in a yellow hat, sitting alone with her cup of coffee in a dingy, deserted cafeteria, is a perfect example.

Friday, May 27

Family movie night. It's Amy's turn. We watch Wes Anderson's *Isle of Dogs* for the second time. The first was when we caught it at the public library when it came out.

Saturday, May 30

In everyday experience, weeks and months somehow evaporate into each other. In normal life, few people seem to be dismayed by this. These days, though, everyone is inside their own COVID brain fog, and we complain about the way time stumbles and sleepwalks us past every new day.

I've taken to reading old diaries, trying to understand how I've arrived at this place. I find a Duo-Tang notebook from when I was 15, and it seems that I would oscillate between depression and religious mania. In one entry I observe: "I think I'm becoming superstitious. Not in the usual way, avoiding black cats, but something worse. I'll hear a voice that tells me: 'if you don't do this, or do that, you won't get to go to Japan and study Zen.' Stuff like having to touch the head of my Buddha statue 5 times when I leave my room. Omens are everywhere. I know it's absurd but I can't stop."

You weren't being superstitious, you poor fuck; you were showing the first signs of OCD.

And then, a few months later: "Guatemala has had some terrible earthquakes. It is estimated that 14,000 have been killed. I, in a sense, seem to need suffering. I almost feel happy to feel sorry for them. I get high on compassion. This, again, is a perverted form of ego. It is really sick. God cure me of it and God help them! Well, I'm tired, and so will meditate and go to bed."

Sunday, May 31

No systemic racism in the U.S., claims a Trump advisor. People protesting George Floyd's murder and wearing masks for COVID, not only in American cities but now in Canada and England too.

My mother, who will turn 81 on this year's Bloom's Day. In too much pain to have a FaceTime conversation with us today. Stenosis.

Our neighbour, a concert violinist, is barefoot in combat pants and black t-shirt and giving an outdoor violin lesson to a girl in a polka-dot dress. The child's mother is holding out her phone horizontally, recording her daughter as she tries to learn how to play what sounds like *La Marseillaise*. All are masked, though the student's is leopard print.

Zindlefarb and scuba nought. A nonsense phrase that I repeated quietly aloud to myself dozens of times today: my form of stimming. A new phrase will suggest itself tomorrow.

Monday, June 1, thru Wednesday, June 3

Saskatchewan eases its lockdown and has opened up its provincial parks to its own citizens: we go camping at Duck Mountain Provincial Park. Campfires are forbidden, so Amy buys an old-fashioned charcoal barbecue with a round lid. Jakob cooks us hot dogs.

Despite ticks, the birding has been wonderful. Eagles, red-necked grebes. Loons. A lone Franklin's gull. A common merganser. Best: the killdeer with 3 chicks. The loons glisten with water droplets. The black their heads retain after diving isn't an ordinary black: it's a preternatural dye that shimmers with refulgent austerity.

Seventy-kilometer-per-hour winds arrive the night of the 3rd, so we decide to return home one day early. South of Melville, as we drive through complete darkness, Amy shouts: "A moose! Stop!" Impossible to stop, so I swerve, just avoiding its back legs. It's a male, his body at least a meter higher than our bug-smeared white car.

A brindled mass flashing in the headlights.

"The human realm is like the tip of a hair on the body of a horse," writes Zhuangzi.

If somewhere along the drive I'd gone two seconds faster, we'd be hospitalized or worse. If the moose had delayed his saunter across the road two to three seconds, the same. I'm shaking as I drive, but I know that my mind will get lazy when it tries to acknowledge this near-event-of-dying: as each day turns into another one, my thoughts will inevitably leave that moment stranded back there on the highway.

Friday, June 5

Laurie Anderson's 73rd birthday. And 31 years ago in Beijing, the Tiananmen Square protests resulted in tanks and bloodshed.

My sister and Kelly, the man who would become her husband, then a med student, were in Beijing in May of 1989 and saw the Statue of Democracy. She sent a postcard of a scroll painting featuring some bamboo that's in front of me as I type.

A single man facing four tanks … where is Tank Man, and is he well? Well and where? And how is it that time is scrubbed clean of what happens? One day COVID will be a memory that's on nobody's playlist, a latent ratio measuring active oblivion: chance.

What is it like to be in Wuhan and remember this day?

Apart from contracting COVID, what concerns me the most is something Camus says about the citizens of Oran once the plague had passed. Denial replaced their earlier fear: "Calmly they denied, in the teeth of evidence, that *we* had ever known a crazy world in which men were killed off like flies."

When a vaccine arrives and life returns to normal, will we carry on as we did before, or will we recognize the societal failures COVID has revealed? This may be my mood disorders speaking, but I don't know if we have the courage to face how flimsy our grasp actually is of what's headed our way.

TO THE PERSON I WILL HAVE BEEN, YESTERDAY

It makes sense that historical circumstances can dictate what's possible for a person, and possibility can sometimes be easy to discern, but how can one determine what choice is (or agency for that matter) when someone has a disability or is mentally ill?

I continually search online for new information about NVLD, and once I came upon the description of a child with the disability who, upon coming home from school, would go straight to his room and shut the door. His parents would ask him what was wrong, and he'd angrily blurt out that he just needed to be alone. He needed to think about things. I recognize this boy because I learned early on that the only time I felt truly safe was when I could isolate myself. What was best was to go into my bedroom, close the door, and open a book. That was then: although the strategy remains the same, I think I can say with certainty that NVLD becomes more acute and worsens as one ages. No studies have been done to illuminate the aging person with this condition because psychologists concentrate on how best to help school-age children.

But if I reconsider this ancient need to be alone and try to determine the genesis of behavior, I find that I have even less agency than I'd supposed when I was first diagnosed. For instance, stacks of magazines and newspapers have accompanied me all my adult life. I brought boxes filled with newspapers when Lynn and I moved from Toronto to

Saskatchewan in 1997. One of them remained until a couple of months ago. Why? Because I hadn't read them all yet, and therefore I hadn't yet been able to grasp what they've been adding to reality. She hasn't, but with her family's experience of OCD, Amy might reasonably call this habit *hoarding*. I see it as an ongoing curiosity. And it's emblematic of how I can never keep up with what's happening.

I've been drawn to philosophy since I was a teenager, partially because philosophy seemed to account for the various perplexities that confronted me: the unfairness of life, the bewildering mystery of time. Marx, Nietzsche, Sartre, and Camus. Each one of them revealing something new, or putting into words what I had only sensed. Epictetus taught me the word *convalescent* because he argues that wise people should comport themselves as though they were convalescents. Eventually Heidegger. Aristotle says that philosophy begins in wonder, and it may for some people, but is my desire to understand things fundamentally an unconscious form of self-defense? From my earliest memories until now, so much of what happens is incomprehensible. Again, from Palombo:

> For children with NLD, the world is a dangerous place—as they have repeatedly found from their experiences. From early childhood, their efforts at negotiating circumstances around them have led to failures or disastrous outcomes.

One theory for the cause of NVLD is damage to the white matter in the brain from blunt trauma to the skull. I wonder what sort of person I would be if I hadn't fallen and struck my skull very, very hard twice when I was a child, once tumbling from several feet onto a concrete floor when I wasn't much more than a toddler and another time falling backwards and striking my skull on an icy hill at school one late afternoon when everyone else had left, a sensation I can still recall. Would I be totally chill? Or even a little chill? Would I still be writing this essay?

Where life makes sense.
   —slogan on the Trans-Canada Highway that welcomes visitors into Swift Current, Saskatchewan

*

Long before I was diagnosed with NVLD, I began reading about depression. If I note that this was pre-Internet, which meant turning to books, this detail isn't meant to offer spurious information. Present-day objects and technologies manifest minute or radical temporal change, and our attachment to them ensures that we tend to perceive the present—that amazing glue to which nothing sticks—to be the core of reality. However, as every depressive knows, things aren't quite that simple. The two books I've found that most intricately discern the metaphysical dimension of depression are Wallace's *Infinite Jest* and Julia Kristeva's *Black Sun: Depression and Melancholia*. When I started reading about depression, *Infinite Jest* hadn't been written yet, but *Black Sun* had. That book showed me how a depressive's obsession with time is, in fact, part of the condition:

> Massive, weighty, doubtless traumatic because laden with too much sorrow or too much joy, *a moment* blocks the horizon of depressive temporality or rather removes any horizon, any perspective. Riveted to the past, regressing to the paradise or inferno of unsurpassable experience, melancholy persons manifest a strange memory: everything has gone by, they seem to say, but I am faithful to those bygone days. I am nailed down to them, no revolution is possible, there is no future.

There are so many ways time can be constituted: time spent shopping; time in handcuffs; the time inside a starving cougar; carving birds to make some money…

Pumas in the Santa Cruz Mountains were being poisoned by mercury in coastal fog.
—"Findings." *Harper's*. February, 2020.

*

If the core of agency eludes me, neither do I grasp the experience of living in a specific historical moment. This past April, I asked Andy what they were going to do now that their journalism classes were done. How would they unwind? Dad, they said, it's 4/20. The only meaningful event I've ever associated with that date was Hitler's birth in 1889, and it was impossible that they would be celebrating that day—they're so far left that in the States they would be labeled as antifa—and so I didn't know the significance of the date to them. They said, *It's the anniversary of Bob Marley's death and so everybody gets really, really stoned today.* A brusque thing, the way anniversaries are tools that are meant to contain what can't be grasped. However, a quick *Wikipedia* search points out that they were wrong: the date has nothing to do with Bob Marley, though it is indeed a day for stoners. Weed, which my generation called grass, is now legal in Canada.

When Marley actually died, on May 11, 1981, Cindy and I were in Spain, having discovered Hieronymus Bosch's *Garden of Earthly Delights.* Days later, she would read in *The Herald Tribune* of a young man in Estonia who starved himself to death in protest of being a political prisoner.

Do those of us formed by the twentieth century experience COVID differently from younger people owing to the numerous movies we saw predicting a pandemic, or the scientists in the news every now and then dressed up as canaries holding warning flags about how unprepared we've been for such an event? Sci-fi no longer, and this one is dangerous (though not as lethal as what may come in the future). I find myself thinking about the twentieth century a lot these days—I always have— but the further we get from it and the younger students become, the more real the century seems to me. This has doubtless been spurred by Jakob becoming interested in the *Planet of the Apes* movies. When we watched the original, I had a brief memory of Charlton Heston cursing the civilization from which he came, ours, for having finally dropped the bomb. But Jakob had encountered this scene through parody in *Futurama.* For me, seeing Heston summoned *Ben-Hur*, Moses, *Soylent Green* (and Jakob knows, from parody once again, that "soylent green is people"), and Michael Moore badgering Heston in the former's anti-gun movie. That the structures of the feeling of a given moment dissipate is commonplace, but what does it mean to think of one's time largely in cultural terms?

Arriving in Florence's train station on an early morning in 1978, backpack (with Canadian flag) on my back, to hear the Bee Gees playing "Staying Alive" in speakers in that ancient station for Christ's sake, instead of say, the Doors. Wondering then about the stupidity of being born a decade too late or too early. Meanwhile, I was entirely missing the deeper history behind all that I associate with my lifetime. Of greater ultimate importance than any cultural artifact or social shift is that we've been living in the so-called Great Acceleration that began in 1945. The rampage that is us ensnaring ourselves in ecological disaster.

Put differently, one sentence can delineate the collapse of an entire ethos, mode of thought, episteme. In Ling Ma's post-apocalyptic novel *Severance*, the narrator is on a "stalk," trying to scavenge supplies from a maggot-ridden house, when she realizes how not only the corpse in the house but also everyone's body, even her own, is corrupted by rampaging bacteria. Desperate, she says, "If I could just find one clean thing here, one thing to please just anchor me." With this simple sentence, the code of existential nihilism portrayed in Hemingway's "A Clean, Well-Lighted Place," or Dirty Harry counting how many bullets he's fired or Jackson Pollock's action paintings—the intellectual and cultural moment in which they contributed and took place—all of this is dispersed. Utterly dispersed. Less overtly hyper-masculine, the modernist phenomenology in Virginia Woolf's *To the Lighthouse* or Sartre's *Nausea* is rendered obsolete by the impossibility of finding sanctuary in Ma's novel. What remains is the future that's already ←

*

If I posited earlier that the personal diary might be the form of discourse most suited to the ongoing experience of subjective time, then today, perhaps the most accurate portrayal of contemporary reality is the graph. Christophe Bonneuil and Jean-Baptiste Fressoz chart socio-economic and earth system trends in their *The Shock of the Anthropocene*: 24 graphs displaying data from population growth to the rise in international tourism to tropical forest loss: each a hockey stick, spanning 1750 to 2010. Each graph the record, not of Hegel's ever-expanding World Spirit, but of a collapsing totality that beggars the imagination. What is it that allows our individual experience to be amplified *just so* over the centuries to have moved us to where we are now, in a situation in which the present is barely present in the present because the future is rewriting and rewiring everything?

*

But I don't get it, embedded in late middle age, I still don't understand anything. Learning about limits, and finitude, the damage that's been done, that I've done. I took an axe to Lynn's life. And when I took Andy to Chicago for Gay Pride in 2013, we spent four days in each other's company, something I hadn't done since I left them, their mother and their brother Jesse ten years before. They were at jubilant ease when we watched the Pride parade, shopping for presents for their girlfriend, wandering around Chicago, they spotting a famous YouTuber, a celebrity entirely unknown to me. After I saw them off in a shuttle to the airport, I returned to the hotel room and realized that not only did I miss them immediately, but I become conscious of the fact that, although we saw each other during each week back home, I'd missed almost all of their day-to-day childhood because I'd chosen another life.

The various orders of chosen grief.

And I get it, I still don't understand the savage inequity of things.

*

To my right is a wooden wand Jakob carved because he's been ripping through *Harry Potter*. And the three of us are going through the movies. Here's an ordinary thing: one component of parental love that my parents and their generation didn't offer was repeatedly watching kids' movies or TV shows along with them—Lord help me when Andy loved the Teletubbies. Here's another ordinary thing: something innate in Jakob has chosen to have him make something tangible from something's he's read: the wand. I've just touched it; the simple smoothness of wood feels as primordial as the first time anyone picked up a stick and decided to remake it with something sharp.

He did this carving while looking into a fire, the wood shavings forming a pile by his feet.

The world never stops looking at us. Does the world need to be seen? There is so much anguish in a piece of concrete, the way the sun happens on top of it, or doesn't, when it rains.

All of this, this thinking about meaning, calculating from history, can become deranged.

*

For decades now, every time August disappears and we find ourselves once more inhabiting the first morning in September, I think hazily about those millions who were alive on this date in 1939—all across North America, Europe, Asia, and parts of Africa—but wouldn't be a few years later because the Nazis invaded Poland on that day. And as November 9 is both *Kristallnacht* and when the Berlin wall came down, I touch this wooden wand, made smooth with Jakob's knife and hands, and I see an endless series of anniversaries. Two new things arising from the Labour Day Weekend of 2004: the father of one of Andy's friends is found dead in his car in an empty parking lot; a school in Beslan is held hostage by Chechen separatists. A massacre occurs. One of the children, a boy who survived being kept in the gym and refused water, waited, kept waiting for Harry Potter to appear, because he knew that he would rescue him and make all things well.

Three male American goldfinches have arrived to feast on Niger seeds in the cadmium-yellow-and-black bird feeder that they may have remembered from passing through here last year. The birds themselves could have flown from a Dutch still life. On a whim, I decide to search Google for Niger seeds so I have a better sense of how long they stay fresh. "The Top 5 Things to Know about Niger Seeds." It's hard to believe that what comes up first is a website called the *Zen Birdfeeder*, a site devoted to the nature we find in our backyards. True story. It's recommended that we adhere to the Zen principles of attention, acceptance, and responsibility.

Who can say what's possible?

A DAY CUT IN TWO

I'm interested in the way a page of writing flies off in all directions and at the same time closes right up on itself like an egg.

—Gilles Deleuze, *Negotiations*

Sunday, May 30, 2021

Returning to Duck Mountain Provincial Park for the first time this season, I wait for a Polaroid to develop. Jakob found the light bulb in the underbrush yesterday, and I've been playing around with it: reflections and ordinary lines shifting a picnic table into something it isn't usually.

These reflections, reminiscent of seventeenth-century Dutch still-life paintings, took a little under three minutes to materialize as the film mutated from a smoky whiteness to the precise image of the glass sphere, the stained, grained wood from which families have eaten. Today's digital Polaroid cameras are much more sophisticated than the originals, and if it's uncanny to watch a photograph quietly emerge either now or in the past, to wait for a Polaroid print to take shape today provides the added weird sensation that something of the twentieth century has also made the trip. This print implicitly contains something not only of the past few minutes, but also of the time when parents would take Polaroids of a birthday party, and then wave the prints around, thinking that doing so would speed up the process. I seem to remember my mother doing this—waving a print in the air—standing in the back yard of our home. At that moment, she was at least three decades younger than I am now.

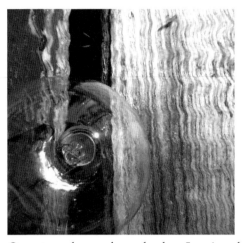

Today her stenosis makes walking on the cement floors of stores such as Walmart too painful, and so she's largely given up shopping trips. When she does go, she uses one of those scooters some stores supply. Last week, she reminded me of a friend of hers who died last year. This friend, Jule, graduated in the same nursing class as Mom did, though she left Ontario and moved to suburban Los Angeles in the 1960s because of the plenitude of nursing jobs in California. We visited her family in 1969, and I was envious of their ranch-style house with its enormous swimming pool. Her boys taught me how to snorkel in it, and the next day we went to the Pacific. (I don't recall seeing any fish, but I did learn that salt water irritates a sunburn, and I was surprised by goops of oil on the beach, the sticky black strands about the size of a baby's curled-up finger.) Apparently, Jule died as the result of smoke inhalation. She was caught alone in her house while a wildfire swept her neighbourhood, strangely stopping at the driveway; she succumbed a few days later.

I hadn't expected to encounter global warming when Mom and I had our weekly chat, but it's almost always here, hovering, ambushing people's private lives on a global scale.

*

I recently participated in a poetry workshop led by Lorna Crozier, and she spoke about the importance poetry grants to silence; as an exercise, she gave us six minutes to imagine different forms silence might take. The ones I came up with—an egg inside a fridge, an empty bathtub dreaming of rain—were a bit easy. This Polaroid, though, has participated in a strange, soundless traffic traversing the human and the machine. The fovea in my eyes took about a tenth of a second to signal the image of the glass bulb to my brain. I decided to take the shot. The camera records the image, and all of this activity remains silent, stays dormant in the picture that I can subsequently circulate online, reproduce in this book, or keep stored in a nearby cabinet. One drawer for Polaroids, another for graph paper, and a third for postcards and souvenirs, including a voodoo necklace I bought in New Orleans. Along with the necklace, I also purchased a shellacked alligator head that day, taken from a large basket full of them by the shop's checkout, only a year before Hurricane Katrina.

I've been unable to experience silence for over a decade because one of the medications I take creates tinnitus as a side effect, a ringing that's here quite literally 24/7. High above the picnic table, fire pit, and wood I've just chopped, there are thousands of midges in the treetops, a feast for an eastern kingbird that dives into their midst every few seconds, their continuous drone similar to what it's like to live inside tinnitus. What the photo doesn't show are the several nearby stumps that were living trees when we set up at the same campsite last year. Only a week after we returned home on that trip (almost hitting a moose as we drove south of Melville toward Regina), a storm tore through the park, destroying several trees and damaging a number of trailers, though no people were harmed. I don't know why, but some of the stumps are cut at about my eye level rather than close to the ground.

This essay requires several beginnings, and I wish that they could take place simultaneously. A Polaroid developing on a wooded peninsula not far from the Saskatchewan-Manitoba border is the simplest one.

*

There's something inaccurate, however, when I said that it's uncanny to watch a Polaroid image appear, the chemical process turning time into a loose representation of memory. The uncanny is fundamentally disorienting, whereas seeing the picture appear out of nothingness is as fun as it's strange. When Jakob presses PRINT on the camera's screen, watches the machine churn out a photograph showing something that's only just happened in front of us, he expresses a cautious delight. There's no delight in the uncanny. A sense of fun may arise *after* the initial contact with the uncanny—Halloween might have this sensation at its core—but the immediate moment of the uncanny is profoundly disruptive. It's one thing to read Freud's essay, which outlines a concept, but it's quite another to experience the phenomenon.

I mentioned earlier that, when I was eating breakfast in Oświęcim's Hotel Galicja, I was startled to hear music from *Twin Peaks* on the café's

Muzak channel. The sudden surprise of hearing something familiar from my deep past, but in an entirely unexpected setting, made me lose my psychic balance. When one experiences the uncanny, the sensation is almost precognitive; it's as if something pounces and is on you before you've even noticed what's happening.

Two days before that Sunday morning, I'd had an even more intense uncanny visitation. I've described how I heard thunder intrude upon on the quietness of the main camp at Auschwitz-Birkenau, but I want to probe more deeply into how the familiar, thrilling rumble seemed very much out of place. It seemed wrong. Thunder is so natural, but there was something in it that day that was not simply harsh, but malevolent. Something fierce was pressing down from the sky, and it was pushing the past up into the present as well. Those of us there in the twenty-first century were stepping into the invisible tracks of other people, tracks that went all the way back to the 1940s. Except that their steps would have dragged. It was as though there was a blurring of temporal horizons, that moment in the camp fusing my own memories of childhood storms with unfamiliar, foreign thunder. The thunder and the very slight wind that came with it carried an imprint of past pain. I don't believe that the uncanny necessarily embodies evil, but it unexpectedly throws open a vacancy inside experience, and it's unclear what lives there, an old memory and/or something external to the self: alien. What's unclear is whether the uncanny exists along a continuum, with varying intensities, or whether an uncanny incident is unique to itself. It is here that the essay begins for the second time.

*

It started with Jakob pranking me yesterday.

We were returning to the campsite, and he told me to stop the car because he'd heard a bird he didn't recognize. We listened. It sounded slightly like a Baltimore oriole, a bird whose song he knows, but it wasn't an oriole. I left the car to investigate. What Jakob had done was find a recording of a nightingale on an app, and he then tricked me into getting out of the car to look for the bird making the familiar, but not entirely familiar, song. (He told me later that he'd chosen a nightingale because he learned that there was no possibility that I'd find one in Saskatchewan.) I went looking for whatever bird had made that song, and, eventually giving up, happened upon an osprey perched on the top of a dead tree.

I'd stupidly forgotten my birding scope, but I was lucky when I glimpsed the osprey that there was a picnic table in the vacant camp-site by the lake. I was able to position my elbow on the table and keep the bird in binocular vision for almost half an hour. We—the bird and I—looked directly at each other several times, and then she went back to taking a break from hunting or nesting.[31] Preened. Stretched. Lived inside a patience that eludes me.

To have a raptor take you in is a special gift. You realize your own irrelevance in such a beguiling way. We get daily reminders of our insignificance, but to be set aside by a hawk is a more elaborate judgment than being ignored or rejected by a person.

It was quite windy, rainy, and when the bird looked toward me, her head feathers would fluff in the harsh wind, making her a hilarious cross between a dinosaur and a punk rocker. As I pondered how utterly differently the osprey and I perceived our surroundings, I wondered if ospreys ever bring to mind other places—the locale to which they migrate in the winter, for instance—and whether they think of these places when they're here at Madge Lake.

I searched its curved beak for the tomial tooth, a small protrusion made of keratin that's used to slice through the spinal cord of prey. Researchers have compared the brains of birds to human beings' and hypothesize that it's likely that we share a similar range of hearing. If this is so, both the osprey and I registered the back-and-forth chattering of the grebes, took in the churn of tires on wet gravel as a truck passed pulling an enormous trailer. But even with my binoculars, the visual world available to the osprey and me is utterly different. Having two fovea in each eye compared to our one, she would be able to discern four different areas of detail simultaneously.[32] I would give a great deal to experience what it's like to be any bird, but especially one like her.

The osprey with the persistent taste of fish on her tongue, the sky a nearby vibration of air, a space so familiar that she couldn't in millennia grasp how differently the primate beneath her perceives the wind high

---

31   The osprey was likely female because she had a so-called "necklace" of brown feathers on her mostly white chest.

32   In *What It's Like to Be a Bird*, David Allen Sibley clarifies: "Look at a single word in this sentence, and then try to read the words around it without moving your eyes. The tiny area of detail in the center of your vision is because of the fovea, a small pit in the retina of each eye where light-sensing cells are more tightly packed.... Most of our visual field, over 110 degrees, is viewed by both eyes.... [A raptor] is seeing four different areas of detail at all times, as well as nearly 360 degrees of peripheral vision!"

above. From the ground, the sky's density looks uniform to me, but a bird must react to abrupt shifts in air pressure and temperature. She then suddenly turned on the dead branch and it was as if the sky was water and she was an Olympic swimmer doing lengths: a small twist of the torso and she was back into being a life with wings, not simply a creature maintaining balance with talons. I watched her disappear through my binoculars.

*

This photo shows what the sky looked like during the drizzle when the osprey and I were adjacent to each other. She was off to the right of the picture. The trees here aren't the way they appeared in reality though. Dead, they were bleached white, slightly more glossy than the white feathers on the bird's chest. As the bird has become a memory, I've been reading to apprehend how other people might have articulated what it meant to watch the osprey.

> The eyes of an animal when they consider a man are attentive and wary.... The animal scrutinizes him across a narrow abyss of non-comprehension.... And so, when he is *being seen* by the animal, he is being seen as his surroundings are seen by him.... Between two men the two abysses are, in principle, bridged by language.
> —John Berger, "Why Look at Animals?" [emphasis in original]

To be seen by one's surroundings: the gathering marsh, a broody grebe on a nest that's mere reeds, woven debris, hardly a structure at all, barely above the waterline. Time not belonging to anyone. Here:

184

a splinter-verse. The pileated woodpecker, not yet arrived, has already passed through yesterday's understory. Meanwhile, a blue-hooded and unmoving rain jacket. Mosquitoes spreading out to detect CO_2, and if the osprey can see down into the lenses of the binoculars pointed in her direction, what images are being conveyed to her brain?

Watching her, I entered a kind of consciousness that made ordinary details—the drizzle, my stiffening elbow, wondering what Jakob and Amy were doing—disappear. Inside this state, I tumbled through several levels of thought. Gradually I let everything go, simply lingered and let the bird's beauty breathe inside.

> Beauty is therefore an *event*, a process, rather than a condition or a state…. Beauty is fleeting, and it is always imbued with otherness. For although the feeling of beauty is "subjective," I cannot experience it at will. I can only find beauty when the object solicits me, or arouses my sense of beauty in a certain way. Also, beauty does not survive the moment of the encounter in which it was created. It cannot be recovered once it is gone. It can only be born afresh in another event, another encounter. A subject does not cognize the beauty of an object. Rather, the object *lures* the subject while remaining indifferent to it.
> —Steven Shaviro, *Without Criteria: Kant, Whitehead, Deleuze, and Aesthetics* [emphasis in original]

The bird *was* beautiful in the way Shaviro describes, but there was something else: her power. Kantian aesthetics says: if the bird was powerful, and if this power pushed past the beautiful, it would then be in the category of the sublime, specifically the dynamic sublime. And that would have the corollary that the bird's magnificence has no external existence; rather, it resides solely within the human perceiver. Countering this, Jorie Graham interjects, disrupting conventional aesthetics. "The sublime is so alone," she writes: "It watches us." If Kant refuses to acknowledge that we can discern anything apart from what we project on to it, Graham points toward something that exists alongside us. But I think her poem also eases us past her metaphor. We must leave behind the integrity of her astute observation that the sublime observes us and go beyond it; the bird was a deepening that both maintained and negated the present, silently eliminating the need for the word *alone* and making the notion of a reciprocal, communal *us* simply an afterthought—

I picked up some wet soil and rubbed it between forefinger and thumb. Try to go beneath associative and logical thought. I find myself mumbling to the osprey. *Bless you, beautiful creature, bless…* and then something unexpected and absurd from deep memory arrives. *You know what*, I tell the bird, squishing the mud: *it's been a long time since I've gotten baby shit on my fingers.*

*

"If, too often, I have the distressing feeling of being separated from nature by a multiplicity of screens, I think it is possible to see these screens reflected in my way of writing." This is Michel Leiris, from *Scratches*, the first volume of *The Rules of the Game*. He doesn't mean virtual screens precisely, as someone would today if they were anxious about digital screens interfering with a response to nature. Yet his trepidation regarding mediation is utterly prescient of the twenty-first century, in this book that was written during the Nazi occupation of France.

*

There was a time when the Canadian $10 bill featured an osprey flying with a fish in its talons on one side and John A. MacDonald on the other. It was issued in 1989, though the flag on the parliament buildings behind MacDonald's face is the one he would have recognized, not the one Canada flies today. The Canadian Mint believes in maintaining the integrity of historical horizons. There was likely one of those $10 bills in my wallet on an evening in June that year when Lynn and I saw a small crowd in Nathan Philips Square protesting the Tiananmen crackdown. We stayed only briefly. Lynn had been a Trekkie since childhood, and *Star Trek IV: The Voyage Home* was playing at an uptown Cineplex at 7:00. She'd worked all week, so off we went, but I still wish we'd skipped the show and listened to what people at the rally had to say.

*

I once saw an osprey, not silently perching, but hovering over the lake and then catching a fish at Duck Mountain. Amy and Andy were in one canoe, Jesse and I in the other. Frida, our border collie, was initially in their canoe, but leapt out because she couldn't stand the pack being separated. This was in 2007. (We had to put Frida down due to dementia last year.) Andy and Jesse were kids, and the particular osprey we saw could have been a parent (or grandparent) of the one I noticed this past May. There were four different kinds of minds at work that early afternoon: the striking bird about to make a kill; the fish aloft, secured tightly within the bird's talons and unable to breathe in the air; a canine's sense of the pack, and my own mind, which was thrilled with the osprey's beauty. But to judge the osprey as visually beautiful has the ethical and epistemological corollary of also recognizing that the materiality of the world—the nerves and neurons present in this tableau—osprey, fish, dog, human—is met inside a domain that mostly lacks a capacity for vision. The canoe, the lake, the sky. Almost all of our surroundings were unperturbed by an incapacity to see or perceive anything at all.

Though to a creature with wings, it might seem striking that almost all phenomena are incapable of flight.

And all of these various things collide within the fish's agony.

*

My eyesight is very poor, but I think that the reason I'm fascinated by the fact that vision is a scarcely occurring phenomenon in the world of weather, the chemicals composing a Polaroid print, and the trees surrounding the marsh is that I could have lost my sight shortly after being born. Only a brief amount of time separates me from medical procedures affecting premature newborns that were practiced prior to my entry into the world. Had I been placed in an incubator only a few years earlier than 1960, it's likely that I would have suffered retrolental fibroplasia, the scarring of tissue that permanently affected the eyes of premature babies who'd been placed in the NICUs of the time. I learned about this horror from reading Annie Dillard, whose mother's hero was a doctor who'd theorized that the condition was caused by pumping too much oxygen into the machines. This practice wasn't stopped until the late 1950s.

I was also allergic to milk. There were fewer non-dairy products available to parents then than now, and it took a few months for mine to find a soy formula that allowed me to eat without screaming. If my unceasing distrust of the environment conceivably began from the distress caused by being in an incubator and feeling awful whenever I was given food, it could have been infinitely worse.

*

Begin again.

The other day I was meditating, trying to merge into the understanding that each breath was the material successor to those breaths I took as a premature baby in an incubator, and that another new breath would subsequently lead to wherever I'll be when my breathing ends.

It began to rain.

Because of Saskatchewan's drought, I got up and went to check that the rain barrels were properly connected. One of them had its lid off and inside it a fledgling house sparrow had drowned. I scooped it out of the rain barrel and laid it down, only to see its beak moving very slightly. There was some crusted yellow where its beak joined its face, but its legs were straightened out 180 degrees behind it, signaling that I'd arrived too late.

It was disturbing to recognize that, as I was reminding myself of finitude, this small creature was fighting not to drown. I couldn't have known what was happening in the barrel, so I'm not culpable, exactly, but I hate to think how terrified the bird must have been. When I returned inside to resume meditating, I imagined how the last few minutes might have appeared to an especially perceptive pair of eyes floating above the back yard, eyes belonging to a sort of spiritual drone. Viewed from this vantage point, my paltry efforts at largely self-taught zazen had the effects of a sun-shower, quenching nothing, and the struggling sparrow gave off the piercing energy of the titanium and magnesium flaring of a sparkler burning, a sparkler held in a child's hand.

The matter escalates.

Aging is ongoing, relentless cognitive decline, and I get daily reminders, some wrenching, others banal. Of the latter, I've recently noticed that I'll start something and not finish it. Taking pasta out of a storage bin, I'll forget to put the lid back on. Amy's in the same boat: we are each aware of the other's memory problems, but we haven't yet gathered the nerve to speak openly about them and determine what we should do. The bird drowned because she'd taken some water out of the rain barrel for her garden earlier, but neglected to replace the lid. If she hadn't forgotten to put the lid back on the barrel, the fledgling would likely be alive.[33] The need to recognize chaos, contingency, and decay

---

33   I forgot to replace the same lid yesterday, despite the fact that I made a mental note to be more attentive.

is woven deeply into Buddhism—and in late middle age these troubles aren't abstractions—but I keep returning to the disparity between the fledgling's experience and my own during that specific half hour. That the sparrow was physically adjacent to me, it straining not to die, me trying to concentrate, embodies the unsettling nature of simultaneity and contingency.

*

I first sensed something of this distressing, bewildering situation during a game of baseball in elementary school. A batter hit what likely would have been a home run, except that after hitting the softball, he let the bat fly backwards, striking the catcher in the teeth. The game ended as the catcher, a friend of mine named Ralph, collapsed, screaming, with blood foaming from his mouth. While kids and the supervising teacher crowded around him, his Mom was at home, likely having her mid-afternoon coffee and cigarette, anticipating her son's normal return from school. Soon her rotary phone would ring with its unforeseeable news. That she didn't know of this accident at the moment it happened seemed wrong to me then. It still does. The accident resulted in Ralph's having permanently rearranged top teeth (dented back at about 45 degrees and never repaired because his family didn't have dental coverage). What happened to him that afternoon also showed me the precarious nature of contingency.

The reason Ralph insisted on playing catcher was because he identified with Schroeder in the *Peanuts* comic strip. Schroeder, who occupied this position on Charlie Brown's team, was also a genius at playing Beethoven on his toy piano. Because Ralph took much pride in having been born on Beethoven's birthday, he emulated Schroeder. Beethoven meant nothing precise to me, but presumably Ralph was informed of the shared birthday by his Austrian parents, who came to Canada shortly after the war. If Ralph had been born a few days on either side of December 16, he might not have been playing catcher that day. Eventually he became a connoisseur of rock music, assembling an array of LPs that surpassed anyone's music collection I've seen since, though with streaming, having a personal library like that isn't meaningful any longer. It was from him that I first heard T-Rex, King Crimson, and the Sex Pistols, music made far away from southern Ontario. His family life was difficult, so he did small things like getting unusual pets to shore up a sense of self. He had a tarantula and a fragile (then difficult to find)

Venus flytrap. One evening he'd had to work at convincing his mother not to get rid of the spider when it bit her on the neck, though it was her fault because she'd allowed it to sit on her shoulder and ignored the potential danger when it started climbing up toward her face.

Ralph's gone now, but I don't know what happened to him. When my mother worked as a nurse in the town clinic, she knew everything about everyone, but she's been retired for almost twenty years. There's nothing about Ralph's death on the Internet. Rumour has it that he died of lymphoma. Those hundreds of LPs are likely in a landfill. The way I die could possibly be related to Ralph: before initiating me into smoking marijuana, he told me that, in order to get used to the harsh smoke, I should start smoking cigarettes. Getting high with weed only mattered to me for a few years, but I was addicted to nicotine for thirty.

*

I've been finding it difficult to resume daily meditation because of the sparrow, though feeling this way is ethically sloppy. Extrapolating from the drowning bird whose plight was hidden from me to situations of which I *am* informed—such as the likelihood of refugees trying to cross the Mediterranean in unseaworthy craft as I type this sentence—means that the incompatibility of my experience with that of others should always disturb me when I measure breaths. (I once raised this issue with my meditation teacher, and she said that meditation is a non-violent activity that usually results in a person becoming more compassionate. Fair enough, and possibly true, but.) Whether one gives to reduce guilt or simply to offer help, it's easy to make a donation to any number of charities that aid refugees. (Though the amounts I donate never inconvenience me.) When one clicks *submit* on the Doctors Without Borders website, however, the ungraspable pain in the world opens up instantly → to think of the grief that engulfs refugees expands to those other people requiring medical research, and also to the untold trillions of life forms lost to habitat destruction. If the world has always engaged disparity—the *Dhammapada* asking, "Why is there laughter? Why is there joy although (the world) is always burning?"—the scale of this burning has become more immense, literally and metaphorically. The Great Acceleration began roughly when T.S. Eliot published *Four Quartets*, his farewell to writing poetry. Consider that the stillness in an abstract Chinese jar to which Eliot refers in "Burnt Norton" has turned into Ai Weiwei's porcelain pillar, six interconnected vases, three meters tall, portraying what happens continuously to people

190

across the world. If ospreys would be indifferent to the drowning house sparrow fledgling → neither would they be capable of behavior that would make others flee their homes.

Ai Weiwei, *Vases with Refugee Motif as a Pillar.* Gardiner Museum, Toronto. (Taking photographs was encouraged for the show *Unbroken*, 2019.)

During the saddest moments in our history, mankind has had to prove their worth as humans to their own kind.

—Ai Weiwei, *Humanity*

*

"Dead elephants," Francis Bacon told Peter Beard, "are more beautiful because they trigger off more ideas in me than living ones. Alive, they just remain beautiful elephants, whereas the other ones are suggestive of all types of beauty."

Francis Bacon requires another beginning—

While the osprey had a much better sense of the environment that surrounded us, she wouldn't comprehend the behavior that led my historian friend Philip to spend the winter eagerly studying Peter Beard's 1977 aerial photograph series of elephant corpses. (First exhibited in the late 1970s, they're currently being shown in London's Ordova Gallery alongside paintings by Bacon.) I don't mean to be glib by stating that a raptor doesn't have an understanding of scholarship, photography, an art show in London, or Bacon's problematic sense of beauty. It's impossible to know everything about birds. Does contemporaneity mean anything to them? Does this female osprey feel concern for her chicks when she's not around to protect them? Does she have a theory of mind to evaluate the bald eagle who competes with her for fish? We don't know.

We'll never know.

COVID deprived Philip and me of our conversations at the university and the walks we'd taken in all seasons around the east part of Wascana Lake by the Science Center, along the trail where I'd seen the night heron in 2017. In addition to avant-garde Japanese photographers, he's been fascinated by Beard's work and has been attempting to determine how the elephant photos were taken, what sort of plane Beard was in when he shot the images. When we went for a walk in late spring 2021, he mentioned that Bacon had fallen for Beard. I haven't seen enough of Bacon's work to have an opinion on it, though when Philip referred to him, I recalled some brutally haggard self-portraits. I'd seen them in New York a week after Cell 23. They showed me a visual correlative to what I'd felt like—no, to what I'd *been*—inside.

If contingency can inflict havoc on an unsuspecting life, it can also occasion serendipity. After I'd returned from the walk, I discovered an article describing the Beard-Bacon show. The gallery has a link to an article titled "The Safari of Horror," the source of the epigraph for this section. Also, this remark by Bacon: "I once saw a bad car accident on a large road and the bodies were strewn about with broken glass from the car, and the blood and various possessions, and it was in fact very beautiful."

There's something equally evocative and disturbing about that evaluation, and it makes me realize how little I understand what constitutes beauty. If I take Bacon seriously—that is, look past his desire to be contrarian—and consider the accident scene in strictly formal terms, then perhaps Bacon could be embodying a shift in historical values. Unlike the ideals of beauty promulgated by a classicist such as Sir Joshua Reynolds, perhaps Bacon relished the random, chaotic nature of the accident, the violent contrast of flesh against pavement, the colours derived from the human body versus industrial paint. But how can one sidestep content in this case? The referent is inextricable from the formal beauty.[34] If Bacon succeeds in redefining beauty, he would likely denigrate me for sentimentality. Perhaps he'd be right to do so. I sometimes think that the dead

---

34   Is there a connection between Bacon's aesthetic and his politics? In *The Art of Cruelty: A Reckoning*, Maggie Nelson quotes Bacon: "I'm not upset by the fact that people do suffer… because the differences between people are what have made great art, and not egalitarianism."

animals in a traditional still life embody a cost to being in a way that differs from the partially unpeeled and resplendent lemons (so beloved by Dutch genre painters) that often accompany the carcasses. (And yet, I don't have the resolve to quit eating meat entirely.) Kant can go nowhere from beauty but to the sublime, and are we to perceive the elephant corpses and the traffic accident as versions of the sublime? These images (and their corresponding realities) loosely fit the dynamic sublime, but isn't there also a degree of schadenfreude in both, especially the car crash scene?

Serendipity: I've only now noticed that the back cover of Leiris's *Scratches*, which I began reading before I went for the walk with Philip, has a blurb from Bacon: "For me his work is not only a document that enriches our knowledge of man, but also a personal testament that touches me deeply." More serendipity: a reference to Bacon in Shaviro's *Without Criteria*, a book that I started reading weeks ago as well:

> As pure, contentless [*sic*] communicability, beauty is also a pure effect, divorced from its rational and material causes…. Bacon conveys this point well when he says that, in his paintings of "the human cry" he "wanted to paint the scream [itself] more than the horror" that provoked it. Bacon's scream paintings are disturbingly beautiful, all the more so in that the situations to which they refer are not.

After talking with Philip, it feels as though Bacon has been pressing in my direction for weeks, but unlike him and Shaviro, I'm disquieted by the seeming fissure between the beautiful object and the violence from which it has been displaced. Philip described the elephant photographs as embodying "carnage," and it seems to me that we need to conceive of an aesthetic that borders carnage, the beautiful and the sublime, the uncanny and often the abject, but that can't be reduced to any of these. It was with the osprey that I sensed this force: there was something within and emanating from the bird that flashed like lightning among these various aesthetic modalities, showing their outlines and then borrowing (as it were) something of their qualities, but ultimately remaining separate from them, resisting codification. It's volatile, this force that the osprey emanated, something rogue that can be perceived, but not conceptualized.

The photographer and painter are dead; what remains are the images each man made. Presumably the elephant corpses Beard photographed are gone as well. Yet, the Beard-Bacon show suggests how the present is crammed with invisible cylinders of the past. We can't know whether the osprey's present is similarly constructed. I've occasionally noticed an eagle posted on a tree near the marina's boathouse a few hundred meters from where I sat alongside the osprey that day. Does she retain the other bird's image on the dead branch when the larger bird isn't there? Does she maintain the sense of what it's like to fly within a sky dense with the particulates from forest fires coming from across the lake, fires that worsen every year?

Let me shift direction once more.

*

On an impulse you watch a stream of water bleed off the counter, which is what writing the present amounts to anyway.

—Lauren Berlant and Kathleen Stewart, *The Hundreds*[35]

35   Since I started reading Berlant, I've checked every few months to learn whether she's published anything new. What I didn't know on May 30 was that she was dying of cancer. Last week a friend told me she'd succumbed at the end of June 2021. We need a word that isolates what it's like to return to the works of a well-loved author, knowing that they are a contemporary, and another that details the subtle shift that transpires when the writer has recently died. The words on the page look identical, but they're different. This situation is quite unlike reading books written by the dead. When one reads Kant's *The Critique of Judgment*, one continually keeps in mind that he'd never learn how a painter like Bacon would complicate his conception of the beautiful.

Back at the campsite, Jakob's sitting in a collapsible chair reading Victor Hugo's *Les Misérables*, and I ask him what page he's on. 225. Having told me that the narrator has found himself exploring the landscape where the battle of Waterloo had been fought, Jakob doesn't know that I've deliberately taken journeys because I've wanted to see places that were part of the daily lives of certain artists or writers. The pharmacy in New York where Joseph Cornell purchased items to place within his Magic Boxes; a street Etty Hillesum often cycled down during the 1940s. The fields Van Gogh saw outside of Arles. In my backpack on the picnic table: a diary, some Polaroid film, a field guide to birds, and *Voices from Chernobyl: The Oral History of a Nuclear Disaster* by Svetlana Alexievich. The latter's because I've recently been trying to learn about things that happened when I was younger, but didn't think much about at the time.

Just after the Chernobyl disaster took place in 1986, Lynn and I visited a friend who worked for the Canadian government as a chemist in Ottawa. He'd been testing milk products for radiation levels, and not wanting to waste food, served us a variety of cheeses he'd determined in the lab were safe. There was radiation present in them, but it was at an acceptable level, he claimed. He was having fun, challenging us to eat the cheese.

Trying to grasp something of the enormous difference between what was in front of me in Ontario versus what was happening in Russia in 1986, I realize that, with each interview Alexievich conducts, I learn a different shade, a different texture of what's impossible to understand. Something simple: Lynn and I married in 1985; after the accident, numerous women, some newlyweds, desperately tried to gain admission to hospitals in which their husbands were rapidly disintegrating because of radiation poisoning. These men had either worked at the plant or were first responders. One woman recalls that, before the accident, she'd go to sleep holding her husband's hand, something that Lynn and I did as well. She held his hand in the hospital too, but eventually pieces of his skin would cling to hers when she removed it.

in spite of everything
we are our brothers' keepers

ignorance of those who are lost
undermines the reality of the world

—Zbigniew Herbert, "Mr. Cogito on the Need for Precision"

If our responsibility to others pertains to ethics—and is thereby a claim that can be disregarded, even contested—then Herbert's second assertion—that being unaware of others "undermines the reality of the world"—speaks to a metaphysical obligation that is less easily disputed. Alexievich cites a certain Pyotr S., a psychologist who'd been a child during the war and had gone to the Chernobyl zone several times. "Memories are very fragile things, ephemeral things," he observes; "this is not exact knowledge, but a guess that a person makes about himself." I'm completely taken aback by his notion that a memory is a guess, a supposition one makes about oneself.

—If memories are merely guesses, conjectures, or possibly predictions, what's involved when we keep returning to those details that are lodged inside us? Are we gamblers then or actuaries?—

Fascinating as this man's ideas are, Herbert would insist that I must admit Pyotr S.'s life into my own, learn something of how trauma has shaped him.[36] Herbert, I think, would admit that, prior to my reading Alexievich's book, there was no possibility I could have had any knowledge of Pyotr S.'s experience. The poem's aphorism would seem extravagant, then, even illogical. But doesn't that miss the point? To encounter the lost invites grief, a force which, pressing upon us, opens the world. Grief should be contagious. That it isn't— and that no one can extend empathy sufficiently—doesn't detract from the poem's plainly stated challenge that its reader acknowledge "the lost." How Herbert's reader reacts to this challenge depends on the individual, but the poem doesn't say that ignoring the lost diminishes the reader's perception of the world's reality. Rather, the world's reality is *itself* sapped. How can this be? The totality of the world's phenomena exists independently of any person; the (presumed) brute violence that causes people and other life forms to be lost is a more fundamental reality than any textual representation of it.[37] Difficult as it is to conceive, reality, according to the poem, is independent of the present. Our task, it would seem, is to learn how to recognize the

---

36   Pyotr S. mentions how, when he was a child, women would take him and other children to a sauna. There, he saw that the women's uteruses "were falling out, they were tying them up with rags. I saw this. They were falling out because of hard labor. There were no men, they were at the front, or with the partisans… the women carried all the loads themselves…. When I was older, and I was intimate with a woman, I would remember this…. I wanted to forget. Forget everything."

37   On Auschwitz, Jean Améry writes: "In other words, nowhere else in the world did reality have as much effective power as in the camp, nowhere else was reality more real."

lost: to recognize continually that what's in front of us isn't what's in front of us.

*

After knocking the logs about in the fire, Jakob asks me what it was like when I was a kid. This is the first time he's asked me this, and the question is entirely different from him wanting to know what *I* was like as a child.

Are all children philosophers?

Responding to a child's questions is one way of sending a probe into what constitutes the contemporary, to gauge its unsteadiness.

I don't know how conscious kids are of this question's complexity, based as it is on the intuition that reality changes, and alongside that inference, the faith that the differences can be communicated. Recognizing the impossibility of answering the question with any accuracy, I put the Alexievich down and mentally run through a variety of differences: getting on a bike to buy a comic book in a variety store with my allowance versus playing Mario Bros. on a Switch with friends. Or my repeated nightmare of nuclear war versus current fears of global warming. Or that the only fruit we ate was seasonal while the grocery store today is like the Calgary zoo in its imported variety. Or that there were no public protests by anti-vaxxers for polio, measles, and chicken pox, but today we have neighbours across the street who refuse the COVID vaccine. Instead, I give him two easy answers. *Like you and most other kids,* I told him, *I loved dinosaurs, but back then, no one knew why they went extinct.* It wasn't until the 1980s that the asteroid theory was developed.[38] *So, that's one difference: dinosaurs were more mysterious then, and that was really, really fun. The other thing that was different is movies,* I said. *We could only watch them in a way you'd hate. Unless we got an adult*

---

38   I learned about dinosaurs from a series called *The How and Why Wonder Books*. The one detailing dinosaurs had illustrations by Charles R. Knight. The original murals are in the Field Museum in Chicago. Contingency and the uncanny make their appearance again. After we'd gone to the Gay Pride Parade in Chicago in 2013, Andy and I wanted to go to the Shedd Aquarium, but the lineups were too long. We went instead to the nearby Field Museum, and saw the Knight paintings, images I'd seen hundreds of times as a child but hadn't thought about in decades. It is because happening upon them unexpectedly gave me a slight buzz of the uncanny—rather than the massive jolt that occurred at Auschwitz—that I suspect the uncanny occupies a continuum. What it impossible to discern, however, is whether any given instance of the uncanny is *qualitatively* different from others.

to take us to a movie theater, the only movies we could watch were the ones that TV offered that night. We could only choose among different stations' offerings, and then they were available only at a specific time. (I still find myself dreaming about having to make a choice about which channel to watch. Oddly, I'm holding a remote in these dreams.) *But you, all you need to do is go online, and you can see almost any movie anytime or anywhere. Choose one: you could watch it now. You could watch* Les Misérables *right here in this campsite.*

That was enough; he didn't need any more. He went back to Jean Valjean.

*

Something I've since told Jakob about what it was like when I was young comes from his half-sibling. Andy has told me that, stranded as a child growing up in straight Saskatchewan, without the Internet letting them become connected to other gay kids, they'd have lost it. As soon as they told me about this part of their life, I thought back immediately to a friend of mine who, shortly after coming out as gay in his early twenties, was rejected by his family and committed suicide. Of all the people I've known who have died, most have taken their own lives. Given my age, this pattern will soon shift, but more than half of those people I've known who killed themselves were gay. Today it's a little bit easier not to be straight—in some places, I tell Jakob.

*

There are other differences that contribute to what Raymond Williams calls an historical moment's "structures of feeling."[39]

—The times I spent solo with my father were primarily when we watched World War II movies together. Jakob has never seen a war movie. When I was a boy, it was considered normal for boys to play with toys that imitated war: I had several GI Joes, cowboy guns, swords, even a plastic machine gun. Jakob has a finely crafted slingshot that he ignores. Toys manifesting such violence are now frowned upon by most parents, but movies today are more intensely gory than the ones I saw.

---

39   For a blog post that takes up the question of describing the present to future children by focusing on COVID, see Sara Benincasa's "Those Were Our Years": https://sarajbenincasa.medium.com/these-were-our-years-f42abe1a05de.

—Anger. The prevalent mood that is manifested communally today (by both the right and left) is unalloyed anger. When I saw angry adults, they were pissed with each other. Wives and husbands, neighbours on occasion. Public anger flared, certainly, as the civil rights movement gained visibility and then became contested in the U.S., as shown on TV. But there was no social media to channel and encourage this anger. So, for me, anger among adults was momentary rather than systemic.

When I was Jakob's age there was the *new* understanding that ordinary people could travel if they chose to do so. Eisenhower had finished his highway system, tents and trailers could be purchased for trips to newly opened campgrounds, and flights could be taken to other continents owing to cheaper airfare. There's a difference in tone between the two historical moments—Jakob's and my own as a child—bitterness and grievance spread across the entire population versus the thrill of the journey, an exposure to the new.

—Porn was a *Playboy* magazine (though a friend showed me the small projector his father kept in his workshop to watch movies involving bestiality, ordered from West Germany). Today, porn is [fill in the blank]. Again, the difference is effort.[40] It once took a bit of oomph to procure porn. And again, similar to movies, this generational difference includes increased violence.

—To come at this from another angle: when I started university in 1981 at York University, humanities and social science students were encouraged to read Frantz Fanon's *The Wretched of the Earth* alongside Gaston Bachelard's *The Poetics of Space*.

---

40   This isn't to say that I think that there was any virtue inherent in waiting for movies, though I'm not a psychologist capable of assessing the neurological changes the Internet creates in developing brains. Like coming across an osprey, instant accessibility can be a gift. The Toronto Metropolitan Library once employed researchers who would answer questions asked either in person or over the phone. It would take a couple of hours for one of them to reply to the question "what day of the week was November 30, 1943?" Learning of the occasion in 1970 when Chancellor Willy Brandt unexpectedly went to his knees in Warsaw to apologize for the German brutality inflicted on Poland during the war, I was able to find a YouTube video of the event immediately. Jakob's generation might not understand what it's like for a digital migrant to replay something of what was woven into 1970, to try to discern in the faces what the event entailed. Until then, 1970 for me was mostly confined to my personal memories, and pre-Internet, the determination it would have taken to find a way of viewing Brandt's gesture would have been daunting.

If we go deeper into daydreams of [birds'] nests, we soon encounter a sort of paradox of sensibility. A nest—and this we *understand*—right away—is a precarious thing, and yet it sets us to *daydreaming of security*.

A national culture under colonial domination is a contested culture whose destruction is sought in systematic fashion. It very quickly becomes a culture condemned to secrecy.

Bachelard versus Fanon (and only one has lasted)

My professors, almost all American or British men, tended to agree on what we needed to know: Nietzsche's *The Birth of Tragedy*, Dostoyevsky's *Notes from the Underground,* and Freud's *The Future of an Illusion* were each assigned as required reading in three separate first-year courses I took. Today there's little overlap in disciplines and specific texts (or even writers) are rarely identified in the discussion of what constitutes cultural literacy. Jakob's grandparents (all formed from deep within the twentieth century) continue to assume that their grandchildren will each earn at least one degree. I doubt whether universities as we know them will last much more than another two decades. Maybe three at most. When I think of the possibility of my kids having children of their own, of the lives these people might face, I panic. Will a broken civilization turn most people into peasants and soldiers?

*

Panic about the future rarely leaves. It was intermittently present when I was with the osprey. While I worried about her and her family's future, I watched a male red-necked grebe bring soggy strands of reeds to the female, who was nesting on hardly anything substantial at all on the lake, the place where she was protecting their eggs. Her descendants will likely resemble her ancestors: this small part of Madge Lake was and will be imprinted on all of the individuals hatched here, and it is here that they must return each spring.

Natality.

The osprey stayed on the branch and I began to think of my father.

*

The weekend of May 30 turned complicated with an event faced by most families. My sister in Ontario texted to say that our eighty-two-year-old father wanted to call an ambulance Friday morning because he felt weak and couldn't move from the reclining chair he had slept in the previous night. She dissuaded him from making the call and went to help, but it's clear that he'll likely soon need to move to a retirement home. As I sat on the picnic table, getting a little stiff, I thought about my sister's remark that Dad had hit the wall.

Someone generous with his time and loyal, Dad seems to me one of the luckiest human beings who has ever lived. Born in 1939 in Canada and not born Jewish in Poland in the same year, his father was too young to fight in the first World War and too old for the second. When he graduated with a BA at age 22, he opened a map of Ontario and asked my mother where she wanted to live: teaching jobs were everywhere. When I mention this scenario to today's students, it is beyond their comprehension as they consider their own precarity. Retired at 58, he made more per year with his pension than I did for the first several years of teaching.

The thing is, like most of us, at some point he learned to coast. Apart from the women I've loved, no one has shown me more.

At least one of three criteria has to be met for a person to survive: one needs to be useful, to be loved, to be safe. Old people, like the children of the poor, are often deprived of all three.
—Fanny Howe, *Night Philosophy*

1.
   Dad had a successful career as a teacher and administrator, made several close friends, and then volunteered for Habitat for Humanity upon retiring, but he's recently bemoaned that he doesn't contribute anything anymore. His weeks are often filled with medical appointments, and he's told me he feels he's a drain on the system.

2.
   His most recent girlfriend (with whom he's wintered in Florida) harshly dumped him a few days ago, saying she can no longer care for him because when he falls, she isn't strong enough to lift him upright.

This past Sunday he reiterated his belief that she's thrown him under the bus.

3.

Although he believes that he'll get better, time suggests otherwise. He can't read anymore, so TV is his primary companion.

*

To wonder about one's father's life while gazing at an osprey is to tip into the atavistic.

Questions such as "how does one find a good way to live?" and "how can one prepare for decay?" sift in and out with the impossibility of grasping that the bird now turning its head, its tuft of feathers momentarily blowing up in the wind, is largely the same as its ancestors from the Pleistocene. I wished that my father could have sat with me across the picnic table, but not the man he is today; rather, someone much younger than me now, say, in his mid-30s. I wouldn't give this younger man practical advice about decisions the older man now regrets; instead, I'd ask him about our capacity for ambition and also delusion. Something I've always wanted to know, but have never asked him, is: does everyone have a bullshit detector? That is, when I'm lying to someone, or more pointedly, when I'm deceiving myself, there's this little voice way down at the bottom of a deep stairwell inside my soul that notifies me of the deceit, mocks and rebukes me. This doesn't mean that I'll listen to it and change my tune ... but it's there, nonetheless. I assumed that everyone had this interior judge until I entered academia and met people who made me wonder whether it was possible for someone to lie to him or herself so thoroughly that the little voice I've described is silent or possibly even nonexistent. I'd ask Dad if he had a bullshit detector. Felt he needed one. Or not.

*

Dad once sent me an email with a photo. It was of him, Scotch in hand, on the deck of his girlfriend's house in Florida. The temperature was a perfect 80° Fahrenheit in February. There were several great restaurants in the area. P. was an angel, looking after all of his needs. He was in nirvana, he wrote. I wrote back, clarifying the Buddhist use of the word. The next year he sent me a similar email.

*

Who am I trying to fool? It's impossible *not* to deceive oneself. Trust me. The ego just gets more skilled at evading self-reproach.

*

And I ponder how Dad enjoyed being himself for decades, and now he doesn't.

What I don't understand is how to patch the utter majesty of the osprey onto this sadness.

She flew away across the lake, and I watched her disappear through my binoculars. I sat for a while more, then wandered around the marsh and for reasons I can't discern felt more serene then than I have for decades—all the while I'd been taking medication, exercising, frying kale—but that time with the osprey, fifteen minutes less than a standard session with a shrink, seems to have done me more good than the hundreds of hours I've spent with mental-health workers. Somehow it made finitude—Dad's, my own, those of all for whom I care, those whom I don't know—seem... I'm not sure how to put this except in a banal way: I felt as though finitude doesn't only mean death. And I felt lighter than I've ever felt before.

*

If I wish I knew what it is like to be an osprey, I've wanted almost more than anything else to know what it's like to be another person. What would we discover if, when we woke in the morning, we could observe what it means to be another I? From the inside? I know that Kant blusters on this one because he needs to make his system work. We can't know what it's like to be another person, but we can agree on what's beautiful, he says. Or, as Wittgenstein argued, I can never know whether the beetle in my box is the same as what's inside your box when you use the same word. Proust, though, believes that it is only through art that we escape solipsism and learn how others perceive the world.[41] I've read three writers

---

41   From *Time Regained*: "Through art alone are we able to emerge from ourselves, to know what another person sees of a universe which is not the same as our own and of which, without art, the landscapes would remain as unknown to us as those that may exist on the moon."

since that Sunday in May, only one of them an active bird watcher, and each describes feeling an unusual elation upon encountering a hawk.

I am looking out of my window in an anxious and resentful state of mind, oblivious of my surroundings, brooding perhaps on some damage to my prestige. Then suddenly I observe a kestrel. In a moment every-thing is altered. The brooding self with its hurt vanity has disappeared. There is nothing now but kestrel.
　　—Iris Murdoch, "The Sovereignty of the Good over Other Concepts"

We all have been reminded that a day can be cut in two by three seconds of a hunting peregrine and leave you stilled into silence and the memory of each curve of flight. I'd swear, if I were of a more mystical persuasion, that a hunting peregrine changes the quality of the atmosphere, makes it heavier.
　　　　　　—Helen Macdonald, "The Falcon and the Tower"

A bird of prey comes swooping down... and it reminds me of some-thing. But of what? Then I remember. It was during my first visit to the National Gallery of Oslo. I must have been seventeen years old. I walked around the rooms, looked at the paintings, liked them, espe-cially the national romantic ones.... Then I entered the room where Munch's paintings hung. At a stroke, everything paled. This was what it was all about.
　　　　　　—Karl Ove Knausgaard, "Bird of Prey"

　A lyric essay like this one requires not only several beginnings; it also necessitates that I learn something of the immensity of what others have discovered ↔ and then keep scraping away my private preconceptions to see what's happening inside a moment that has never existed before... and then keep revising what I thought I knew.

*

During that weekend at Duck Mountain, we took a holiday from social and conventional media. That meant we didn't know that CBC was reporting how recently developed radar technology had detected the unmarked graves of some 215 children in a former residential school in Kamloops. For all of my adult life I've been puzzled by a fundamental question: if one could condense everything that was happening that moment, everything transpiring on the planet, what would be the predominant emotion, thought, action… but when I was a child I had no idea that children my own age from the Tk'emlúps te Secwépemc First Nation were incarcerated in places like that.

NOTES

All photographs are by the author.

Contours: In Search of Etty Hillesum

I would like to thank Thomas Bredohl for sharing his expertise on Nazism and translations of German with me for this essay (and others).

For the Westerbork deportation schedule, see http://www.holo-caust-lest-weforget.com/westerbork-transport-schedule. The Kleist citation is from *Caspar David Friedrich* by Werner Hofmann. Walter Benjamin provides an analysis of Klee's *Angelus Novus* in Thesis IX (from "Theses on the Philosophy of History") in *Illuminations*. The citation from Wilfred von Oven comes from Laurence Rees, *Auschwitz: A New History*. Other books that were important to this piece are: Danuta Czech, *Auschwitz Chronicle 1939-1945*; Debórah Dwork and Robert Jan van Pelt, *Auschwitz: 1270 To the Present*; Primo Levi, *Survival in Auschwitz* and *The Voice of Memory: Interviews 1961-1987*; Philip Mechanicus, *Year of Fear*; Aad Wagenaar, *Settela*.

A Day Cut in Two

I would like to thank kat Nogue for alerting me to the Benincasa blog. The idea that Nazism "imprinted pain" comes from Charlotte Delbo, *Auschwitz and After*. Regarding the human eye, I consulted Michael F. Land's *The Eye: A Very Short Introduction*. For information on the Peter Beard – Francis Bacon show, see:
https://www.theguardian.com/artanddesign/2021/apr/07/horror-safari-francis-bacon-peter-beard-inflamed-dead-elephants-heart-of-darkness

BIBLIOGRAPHY

Several books—for instance, Etty Hillesum's *An Interrupted Life and Letters from Westerbork*—are referred to several times throughout the book. Their bibliographic information appears in the bibliography for the initial piece in which they appear.

Bodhisattva on a Bicycle
Berr, Hélène. *The Journal of Hélène Berr*. Trans. David Bellos. McClelland & Stewart, 2008.
Flanagan, Owen. *The Bodhisattva's Brain: Buddhism Naturalized*. MIT P, 2013.
Glowinski, Michal. *The Black Seasons*. Trans. Marci Shore. Northwestern UP, 2005.
Howe, Fanny. *The Needle's Eye: Passing Through Youth*. Graywolf P, 2016.
Kenkō. *Essays in Idleness. Anthology of Japanese Literature: From the Earliest Era to the Mid-Nineteenth Century*. Ed. Donald Keene. Trans. George Sansom. Grove P, 1955.
Phillips, Whitney. *This Is Why We Can't Have Nice Things: Mapping the Relationship Between Online Trolling and Mainstream Culture*. MIT P, 2015.
Sebald, W.G. *The Emigrants*. Trans. Michael Hulse. New Directions, 1997.
Taub, Ben. "We Have No Choice." *The New Yorker*. April 10, 2017. 36-49.

When a Glacier Breathes, Johannes, it Releases Ravens

Barthelme, Donald. *Sixty Stories*. Penguin, 1982.

Berlant, Lauren and Kathleen Stewart. *The Hundreds*. Duke UP, 2019.

Bollas, Christopher. *The Shadow of the Object: Psychoanalysis of the Unknown Thought*. Columbia UP, 2017.

Burke, Carolyn. *Lee Miller: A Life*, U of Chicago P, 2005.

Coles, Don. *How We All Swiftly*. Signal Editions, 2005.

Delillo, Don. *Mao II*. Viking, 1991.

Goldberg, Amos. *Trauma in First Person*. Trans. Shmuel Sermoneta-Gertel and Avner Greenberg. Indiana UP, 2017.

Goodman, Peter S. "A Promise to Philippine Farmers Can Kill Them," *The New York Times,* December 29, 2019.

Grief, Gideon. *We Wept Without Tears: Testimonies of the Jewish Sonderkommando from Auschwitz*. Yale UP, 2005.

Hampl, Patricia. *I Could Tell You Stories*. W. W. Norton, 2000.

Harman, Graham. *Speculative Realism: An Introduction*. Polity, 2018.

Kermode, Frank. *The Genesis of Secrecy: On the Interpretation of Narrative*. Harvard UP, 1979.

Leiris, Michel. *The Ribbon At Olympia's Throat*. Trans. Christine Pichini. Semiotext(e), 1981.

LeMenager, Stephanie. *Living Oil: Petroleum Culture in the American Century*. Oxford UP, 2014.

Lingis, Alphonso. *Irrevocable: A Philosophy of Mortality*. U of Chicago P, 2018.

Markson, David. *The Last Novel*. Shoemaker Hoard, 2007.

—. *Wittgenstein's Mistress*. Dalkey Archive, 1988.

Munro, Alice. *Runaway*. Penguin, 2004.

Paterniti, Michael. *Love and Other Ways of Dying*. Dial Press, 2015.

Schlegel, Friedrich. *Philosophical Fragments*. Trans. P. Firchow. U of Minnesota P, 1991.

Zwicky, Jan. *The Experience of Meaning*. McGill-Queen's UP, 2019.

The Sunday Book

Blanchot, Maurice. *The Writing of the Disaster*. Trans. Ann Smock. U of Nebraska P, 1995.

Delbo, Charlotte. *Auschwitz and After*. Trans. Rosette C. Lamont. Yale UP. 1995.

Judt, Tony. *The Memory Chalet*. Penguin, 2010.

Knausgaard, Karl Ove. *My Struggle: Book 1*. Trans. Don Bartlett. Farrar, Straus and Giroux, 2012.

Smith, Zadie. *Feel Free*. Penguin, 2018.

Bruegel's *Hunters in the Snow* ↔ *Konzentrationslager Mauthausen*
Auden, W. H. *Collected Poems*. Ed. Edward Mendelson. Random House, 1976.
Arendt, Hannah. *Essays in Understanding: 1930-1954*. Ed. Jerome Kohn.
Schocken, 1994.
Ashbery, John. *Selected Poems*. Penguin, 1986.
Berger, John. *And our faces, my heart, brief as photos*. Pantheon, 1984.
—. *Portraits: John Berger on Artists*. Ed. Tom Overton. Verso, 2015.
Bernadac, Christian. *The 186 Steps: Mauthausen*. Trans. S. and L. Van Vliet
White. Ferni P, 1978.
Dean, Carolyn, J. *The Fragility of Empathy After the Holocaust*. Cornell UP, 2004.
Freud, Sigmund. *The Future of an Illusion*. Trans. J.A. Underwood and Shaun
Whiteside. Penguin, 2004.
—. *Reflections on War and Death*. Trans. A.A. Brill and Alfred B. Kuttner.
Read Books, 2000.
Gopnik, Adam. *Winter: Five Windows on the Season*. Anansi, 2011.
Hegel, G.W.F. *Phenomenology of Spirit*. Trans. A.V. Miller. Oxford UP, 1977.
Hillman, James and Sonu Shamdasani. *Lament of the Dead: Psychology After
Jung's Red Book*. W.W. Norton, 2013.
Lyotard, Jean-François. *The Differend: Phrases in Dispute*. Trans. Georges Van
Den Abbeele. U of Minnesota P, 1988.
Mueller, Benjamin and Al Baker. "A Mother Slain on a Playground, a Sea of
Witnesses Silent." *The New York Times*. Sunday, January 1, 2017: 14.
Todorov, Tzvetan. *Facing the Extreme: Moral Life in the Concentration Camps*.
Trans. Arthur Denner and Abigail Pollack. Weidenfeld & Nicolson, 1999.
Tararona, Mer. *The Photographer of Mauthausen*. 2018.
Zagajewski, Adam. *Slight Exaggeration*. Trans. Clare Cavanagh. Farrar, Straus
and Giroux, 2017.

Interlude: the various species of time
Baer, Ulrich. *Spectral Evidence: The Photography of Trauma*. MIT, 2005.
Bernstein, Michael André. *Foregone Conclusions: Against Apocalyptic History*.
U of California P, 1994.
Loy, David. *Ecodharma: Buddhist Teachings for the Ecological Crisis*. Wisdom
Publications, 2018.
Palombo, Joseph. *Nonverbal Learning Disabilities: A Clinical Perspective*.
W.W. Norton, 2006.
Pirsig, Roberet M. *Zen and the Art of Motorcycle Maintenance*. HarperPerennial,
1999.
Émile-Zola, François and Massin. *Zola: Photographer*. Henry Holt, 1988.

The Flâneur, Amsterdam, and a Hawk

Baudelaire, Charles. *The Painter of Modern Life.* Trans. Jonathan Mayne. *The Norton Anthology of Theory and Criticism.*2nd Ed. Ed. Vincent B. Leitch. W. W. Norton, 2010.

Bradatan, Costica. *Dying for Ideas.* Bloomsbury, 2015.

Lindwer, Willy. *The Last Seven Months of Anne Frank.* Trans. Alison Meersschaert. Anchor, 1992.

Mechanicus, Philip. *Year of Fear.* Trans. Irene S. Gibbons. Hawthorn, 1964.

Cell 23

Nelson, Maggie. *The Argonauts.* Graywolf, 2015.

Interlude: a slow-paced, though gilded, hysteria

Kristeva, Julia. *Black Sun: Depression and Melancholia.* Trans. Leon S. Roudiez. Columbia UP, 1989.

Schama, Simon. *Rembrandt's Eyes.* Alfred A. Knopf, 1999.

The Guard in the Museum

Adorno, Theodor. *Minima Moralia: Reflections on a Damaged Life.* Trans. E.F.N. Jephcott. Verso, 1974.

Dobb, Edwin. "Nothing but Gifts: Finding a Home in a World Gone Awry." *Harper's.* 337. 2021. (October 2018): 47-54.

Friedewald, Boris. *Paul Klee: Life and Work.* Prestel, 2013.

Glimcher, Arne. *Agnes Martin: Paintings, Writings, Remembrances.* Phaidon, 2012.

Metz, Cade and Adam Satariano. "An Algorithm that Grants Freedom, or Takes it Away." *The New York Times*, Sunday Business, 1, 6-7.

Warzel, Charlie and Stuart A. Thompson. "How "How Your Phone Betrays Democracy." *The New York Times*, Opinion, January 26, 2020:8.

Zuboff, Shoshana. "The Known Unknown." *The New York Times.* Sunday Review. January 26, 2020. 1. 6-7.

Basketball, John Lennon, and a Helicopter

Morris, Ian. *Why the West Rules—For Now: The Patterns of History, and What They Reveal About the Future.* McClelland and Stewart, 2010.

Schama, Simon. *Scribble, Scribble, Scribble: Writing on Politics, Ice Cream, Churchill and My Mother.* HarperCollins, 2010.

Trussler, Andy. "Chlorine Head." *Grain.* 47.4 (Summer 2020): 29-30.

Contours: In Search of Etty Hillesum

Greenman, Leon. *An Englishman in Auschwitz.* Valentine Mitchell, 2001.

Hillesum, Etty. *Etty Hillesum:An Interrupted Life (The Diaries 1941—1943 and Letters from Westerbork*. Trans. Arnold J. Pomerans. Henry Holt, 1984.

Hoess, Rudolf. *Commandant of Auschwitz*. Trans. Constantine FitzGibbon, Phoenix, 2000.

Hoffmann, Eva. Foreword. *Etty Hillesum:An Interrupted Life (The Diaries 1941—1943 and Letters from Westerbork*. Trans. Arnold J. Pomerans. Henry Holt, 1984.

Kroker, David. *At the Edge of the Abyss: A Concentration Camp Diary, 1943-1944*.Trans. Michiel Horn and John Irons. Northwestern UP, 2012.

Rilke, Rainer Maria. *The Notebooks of Malte Laurids Brigge*. Trans. Stephen Mitchell. Vintage, 1985.

Zen and a Dinosaur

Wetering, Janwillem van de. *The Empty Mirror*. St. Martin's, 1973.

May to June 2020… A COVID Miscellany

Camus, Albert. *The Plague*. Trans. Stuart Gilbert. Hamish Hamilton, 1960.

Deleuze, Gilles. *The Logic of Sense*. Trans. Mark Lester and Charles Stivale. Columbia UP, 1990.

Landau, Felix. Diary Excerpts. *The Holocaust: Origins, Implementation, Aftermath*. Ed. Omer Bartov. Routledge, 2015.

Cooper, David E. *Convergence with Nature: A Daoist Perspective*. Green Books, 2012.

Hampl, Patricia. "The Dark Art of Description." *Best American Essays: 2009*. Ed. Mary Oliver. Houghton Mifflin, 2009.

Kang. Han. *Human Acts*. Trans. Deborah Smith. Hogarth, 2016.

Pastoureau, Michel. *Yellow: The History of a Color*. Trans. Jody Gladding. Princeton UP, 2019.

Thompson, Derek. "What's Behind South Korea's Exceptionalism?" https://www.theatlantic.com/ideas/archive/2020/05/whats-south-koreas-secret/611215/

Walpola, Rahula. *What the Buddha Taught*. Evergreen, 1962.

To the person I will have been, yesterday

"Findings." *Harper's*. 340. 2037 (February 2020): 96.

Ma, Ling. *Severance*. Farrar, Straus and Giroux, 2019.

A Day Cut in Two

Alexievich, Svetlana. *Voices from Chernobyl*. Trans. Keith Gessen. Dalkey Archive P, 2005.

Améry, Jean. *At the Mind's Limits*. Trans. Sidney Rosenfeld and Stella P. Rosenfeld. Indiana UP, 1980.

Bachelard, Gaston. *The Poetics of Space*. Trans. Maria Jolas. Beacon P, 1994.

Berger, John. *Selected Essays*. Ed. Geoff Dyer. Vintage, 2003.

Deleuze, Gilles. *Negotiations*. Trans. Martin Joughin. Columbia UP, 1995.

Fanon, Frantz. *The Wretched of the Earth*. Trans. Constance Farrington. *The Norton Anthology of Theory and Criticism*. 2nd Ed. Ed. Vincent B. Leitch. W. W. Norton, 2010.

Herbert, Zbigniew. *The Collected Poems: 1956-1998*. Trans. Alissa Valles. Ecco, 2007.

Howe, Fanny. *Night Philosophy*. Divided P, 2020.

Knausgaard, Karl Ove. *Autumn*. Trans. Ingvild Burkey. Penguin, 2017.

Macdonald, Helen. *Vespers*. Hamish Hamilton, 2020.

Leiris, Michel. *Scratches*. Trans. Lydia Davis. Yale UP, 1997.

Murdoch, Iris. *The Sovereignty of Good over Other Concepts. The Lesley Stephen Lecture*. Cambridge UP, 1967.

Nelson, Maggie. *The Art of Cruelty: A Reckoning*. W.W. Norton, 2011.

Proust, Marcel. *In Search of Lost Time*. Vol. 6. Trans. Andreas Mayor and Terence Kilmartin. Modern Library, 2003.

Shaviro, Steven. *Without Criteria: Kant, Whitehead, Deleuze, and Aesthetics*. MIT, 2012.

Sibley, David Allen. *What It's Like to Be a Bird*. Alfred A. Knopf, 2020.

Weiwei, Ai. *Humanity*. Ed. Larry Warsh. Princeton UP, 2018.

ACKNOWLEDGMENTS:

This collection has been composed over some difficult years. Without the ongoing support of Amy Snider, my partner, and my children, Andy, Jesse and Jakob, I wouldn't have been able to complete the book. These essays are dedicated to them. And I further dedicate the book to birds everywhere.

Many friends over the years have been generous to read drafts of these essays. Let me especially thank Thomas Bredohl for his expertise in Nazism; additionally, kat Nogue and Dan Tysdal spent time going over individual essays, helping me make them clearer. Susan Lohafer, likely the most gifted reader I know, has blessed me with a delightful and intricate conversation about literature, ethics and the world that goes back for decades. I treasure the long talks I've had with Ben Salloum, his erudition and wide-ranging intelligence have helped me understand my subject matter more deeply. This book would quite possibly not exist without Philip Charrier, a colleague and friend who has continuously supported these particular essays and taught me much about voice. Some others—Derek Brown, Paul Endo, Ray Pekrul, Jeremy Stewart, Drs. Udoh and Pitariu, and Ken Wilson—have offered their wisdom when times became hard.

Additionally, parts of this manuscript were improved by two Writers-in-residence at the Regina Public Library: Trevor Herriot and Jill Robinson; my thanks to them.

Decades of teaching at the University of Regina have allowed me to interact with many wonderful students, too numerous to name individually. I would, though, like to offer thanks to Joel Blechinger, Jeremy and Jesse Desjarlais, and Sarah Fahie for their thoughtful, indeed sparkling emails and helpful reading recommendations. The English Department's willingness to allow instructors to develop their own idiosyncratic courses has enabled me to combine teaching with research and writing.

I also wish to thank Jim Johnstone; his steady, generous support and excellent guidance have helped me turn a rambling collection of essays into this book. And thanks, too, to Theo Hummer for a careful, thoughtful copy-edit. Ellie Hastings did a superb job with lay-out, having to navigate my wonky line breaks and photographs.

Some of the material in this collection has appeared in different forms in the following journals and presses: The Alfred Gustav Press, *Queen's Quarterly*, and *Vallum*. My thanks to the editors for permission to reprint.

Michael Trussler writes poetry, short stories, and creative non-fiction. He is also a photographer. He's published various books, most recently *Rare Sighting of a Guillotine on the Savannah* (Mansfield Press, 2021). His prize-winning work has appeared in domestic and international anthologies and journals. His collection of short stories, *Encounters*, won the Book of the Year and City of Regina Awards from the Saskatchewan Book Awards in 2006. *Accidental Animals*, a poetry collection, was short-listed for the same awards in 2007. He teaches English at the University of Regina.